BOOKS BY SAME AUTHOR

2020: *Applied Management: Chief Executive Officers and Managers' Handbook,* Author House Publisher, UK. ISBN 9781728354774

2018: *Contemporary Issues in Taxation.* Author House Publisher, UK. ISBN 978154629109.

2012: *Financial Accounting for Executives, MBA.* Author House Publisher, UK. ISBN 978148178010.

2011: *International Finance for Developing Countries.* Author House Publisher, UK. ISBN 9781456781705.

2010: *Corporate Finance.* Author House Publisher, UK. ISBN 9781456781705.

2008: *Financial Management Skills for Non- Finance Managers.* Learn and Share Publishers. ISBN 9987425127.

RESEARCH METHODS: MASTERS AND PHD STUDENTS HANDBOOK

LUCKY YONA

authorHOUSE

AuthorHouse™ UK
1663 Liberty Drive
Bloomington, IN 47403 USA
www.authorhouse.co.uk
Phone: UK TFN: 0800 0148641 (Toll Free inside the UK)
    UK Local: 02036 956322 (+44 20 3695 6322 from outside the UK)

© *2020 Lucky Yona. All rights reserved.*

No part of this book may be reproduced, stored in a retrieval system, or transmitted by any means without the written permission of the author.

Published by AuthorHouse   11/30/2020

ISBN: 978-1-6655-8266-7 (sc)
ISBN: 978-1-6655-8265-0 (e)

Print information available on the last page.

Any people depicted in stock imagery provided by Getty Images are models, and such images are being used for illustrative purposes only.
Certain stock imagery © Getty Images.

This book is printed on acid-free paper.

Because of the dynamic nature of the Internet, any web addresses or links contained in this book may have changed since publication and may no longer be valid. The views expressed in this work are solely those of the author and do not necessarily reflect the views of the publisher, and the publisher hereby disclaims any responsibility for them.

CONTENTS

About The Author xi
Acknowledgement xiii
Foreword xv
Dedication xvii
Preface xix

Chapter 1: General Guidelines On Academic Research 1

1.1 Introduction 1
1.2 Book Objective 2
1.3 Common Guidelines 2
1.4 Length of your Research Work 3
1.5 Conclusion 3

Chapter 2: Working With Your Academic Supervisor 4

2.1 Introduction 4
2.2 Getting the most from the supervisory relationship 5
2.3 Mind your Business: It is your work and not your supervisor's! 6
2.4 Dealing with challenges in the supervisory relationship 6
2.5 Conclusion 7

Chapter 3: Developing The Research Topic 9

3.1 Introduction 9
3.2 Formulating a Research Topic 9
3.3 Factors to consider before choosing a research topic 13
3.4 Conclusion 13

Chapter 4: Organizing The Introduction Chapter 15

- 4.1 Introduction 15
- 4.2 Writing the Historical Background of the Research 16
- 4.3 Purpose of the study 16
- 4.4 Defining the Research Problem 17
- 4.5 Stating the Research Objectives 18
- 4.6 Designing the Research Questions 20
- 4.7 Significance of the Research 21
- 4.8 Research Scope and Limitations 22
- 4.9 Organization of Your Research 24
- 4.10 Research Coherence 25
- 4.11 Conclusions 26

Chapter 5: Organizing The Literature Review 29

- 5.1 Introduction 29
- 5.2 Elements of a Research Literature Review 29
- 5.3 Expectations for a Thesis Literature Review 30
- 5.4 Avoiding Plagiarism 31
- 5.5 Standard Citation Formats and Requirements 32
- 5.6 Organizing your Literature Review 35
- 5.7 Theoretical Review 36
- 5.8 Empirical Literature 36
- 5.9 Common mistakes in writing a Literature Review 37
- 5.10 Sources of Literature 38
- 5.11 Conclusion 39

Chapter 6: Conceptual Framework 41

- 6.1 Introduction 41
- 6.2 What is a Conceptual Framework? 42
- 6.3 Objectives of Conceptual Framework 44
- 6.4 Operationalization of the Conceptual Framework Research Variables 44
  - *6.4.1 Key variables in the Conceptual Framework 45*
  - *6.4.2 Independent Variable 45*

	6.4.3 Dependent Variable	46
	6.4.4 Intervening Variable	47
	6.4.5 Moderating Variable	47
6.5	Defining the Measurement of the Research Variable	47
6.6	Challenges in formulating the conceptual framework	49
6.7	Organization of the Conceptual Framework Chapter	50
6.8	Conclusion	51

Chapter 7: Designing The Research Methodology 53

7.1	Introduction	53
7.2	Research Design	54
7.3	Study Population	56
7.4	Study area	57
7.5	Sampling Method	58
7.6	Sample Size	59
7.7	Data Collection Methods	61
7.8	Types of Research Instruments	62
	7.8.1 Questionnaires	62
	7.8.2 Interviews	64
	7.8.3 Focus Group	65
	7.8.4 Observation	66
7.9	Factors to Consider when Choosing Research Instruments	68
7.10	Qualities of Good Research Instruments	68
7.11	Challenges in designing research instruments	69
7.12	Data Analysis	69
7.13	Techniques to Analyze data	70
	7.13.1 Qualitative studies	71
	7.13.2 Quantitative studies	71
7.14	Tools for Data Analysis	72
7.15	Data Presentation	72
	7.15.1 Table Presentation	73
	7.15.2 Graph Presentation	75
	7.15.3 Pie Chart Presentations	77
7.16	Challenges in Data Analysis	78
7.17	Data Reliability	78
7.18	Data Validity	81

7.19	Hypothesis Formulation	82
	7.19.1 Characteristics of good hypotheses	*83*
	7.19.2 Challenges commonly faced when formulating hypotheses	*85*
	7.19.3 Testing of Research Hypothesis	*85*
7.20	Ethical Considerations in Research	86
7.21	Organization of the Research Methodology Chapter	86
7.22	Conclusions	87

Chapter 8: The Research Report ... 91

8.1	Introduction	91
8.2	The Thesis order	91
8.3	Abstract	92
8.4	Research Findings Chapter	94
	8.4.1 Introduction	*95*
	8.4.2 Demographic Information	*95*
	8.4.3 Research Findings for Research Objectives	*95*
	8.4.4 Hypothesis Testing	*101*
	8.4.5 Discussion of the Research Findings	*104*
	8.4.6 Conclusions of the research findings chapter	*106*
8.5	Conclusions and Recommendations—The Final Chapter!	106
8.6	Conclusion	106

Chapter 9: Writing Your References ... 108

9.1	Introduction	108
9.2	Contents of the References Chapter	108
9.3	Conclusion	109

Chapter 10: Thesis Defense ... 111

10.1	Why do theses need to be defended?	111
10.2	Preparing for Defense	112
10.3	Power Point Presentation	112
10.4	Conclusion	121

Chapter 11: Publishing Your Thesis 123

11.1	Introduction 123	
11.2	Converting a thesis into Publishable Paper............................ 124	
11.3	Submitting your paper for journal publication 125	
11.4	Incorporating Reviewer Comments 126	
11.5	Converting a thesis to a book.. 126	
11.6	Conclusion 127	

Appendix 129
    Appendix 1: Sample Published Paper 1 131
    Appendix 2: Sample Published Paper 2 141
Bibliography...149

Also, By Lucky Yona 153

ABOUT THE AUTHOR

Professor Dr. Lucky Yona lectures at Eastern and Southern African Management Institute (ESAMI) in Arusha, Tanzania. He holds a PhD in Finance from Euraka Univeristy in Switzerland, a Doctor of Business Administration (D.B.A.), a master's degree in Business Administration (M.B.A.) as well as a Master of Philosophy (M.Phil.) from Maastricht School of Management (MsM). Professor Yona's undergraduate accomplishments include a bachelor's degree in Commerce and a bachelor's degree of Theology. He is a Certified Public Accountant (C.P.A) and an experienced consultant and international trainer. Lucky has published several finance and accounting books and numerous articles in internationally known, peer-reviewed journals.

Prior to joining ESAMI, Lucky worked with a variety of reputable institutions and companies at the senior management level. Some of these positions included serving as Director of Research and Publication for Esami, Financial Administrator for African Medical and Research Foundation (AMREF), Business Manager for International School of Moshi (now United World Colleges, East Africa), College Bursar for Kilimanjaro Christian Medical College and Chief Accountant at Iscor Mining. In addition to these distinguished positions, Dr. Yona taught Financial Accounting and Taxation at Nyegezi Social Training Institute (now St. Augustine University in Tanzania). He is now involved in teaching various MBA courses at Eastern and Southern African Management Institute (ESAMI) Business School—a prestigious institution serving ten African countries.

ACKNOWLEDGEMENT

My desire to write this book arose from experience of supervising students' working on their master's and doctorate theses and witnessing first-hand the problems and challenges they face. From the thesis proposal stage to the final stages of thesis writing and defending, my students shared their difficulties and deep need for guidance. Many students do not go deep enough when extracting articles from journal publications and don't take the time to publish their theses in book form. Because of these challenges, I thought it would be useful to document some practical aspects of research to guide students through the process. This book tries to explain, in a nutshell, what students should be doing at each stage of thesis development from their initial proposal to their final publishing.

I appreciate the support accorded to me by Karah Germroth for editing this entire manuscript.

I have dedicated this book to my only late daughter, Faith Lucky. Her lifestyle was one of a researcher and a leader. Her inquisitiveness and desire to learn more about everything will always inspire me. I wish she would have lived to accomplish her vision and would have benefitted from the experiences and knowledge documented here.

Professor Dr. Lucky Yona
PHD (Finance), DBA (Banking), MBA (Finance), MPHIL, CPA, BCOM (Accounting), B.Th.

FOREWORD

It is with great honour that i write this foreword in this Research Handbook, not only because I have known Prof Lucky Yona for over 4 years in the academic field, but also in the teaching and consulting field. As both an academic and businessman, l greatly believe in students understanding research as an analytical tool to life's situations. This research handbook still can assist strengthening instructors by learning and appreciating research tools and techniques. Understanding research methods can help students and executives to appreciate the real world in different institutions without prejudice. Many businesses and institutions fail to meet the goals and objectives due to lack of appreciation and use of research work and process.

Lucky Yona has a powerful teaching, supervision career and taking time to put together the Research Handbook is his complete offering to master's and PhD students across the academic horizon. As Napoleon Hill said "you can know yourself only through accurate analysis". Over his long and fruitful carrier Lucky Yona has had numerous opportunities to assess and supervise students' research work, hence a deep understanding of the research requirements for post graduate studies. The Research Handbook becomes then the most practical work to research for post-graduate studies. He has had experience in teaching and supervising both full time and block release post-graduate students and understanding their research needs. Obviously Yona has had great opportunities exploring the philosophy and practice of academic research including the conceptual and theoretical frameworks as they are well explained and illustrated in this handbook.

Remembering our meeting at the MBA Thesis defense for ESAMI students in 2018 in Harare Zimbabwe, we shared the stage as the defense panellists, I listened with admiration and interest as he laid down the proper research procedure for master's students. In this book Yona puts clear examples to new comers in the world of research and outlines the whole research process from choosing a topic, doing literature review, crafting the problem statement, framing research questions, research objectives, writing the theoretical and conceptual frameworks, working on the research methodology (including data gathering and organisation, data processing, analysis and interpretation). Indeed, a powerful tool for research has been produced.

Engaging with this handbook, one will be led in clear paths to the research process for both academic and business environments. Lucky Yona provided empirical evidence that research is indeed necessary for all learning environments both at the Masters and PhD levels.

I hope this book will be a first call of all post graduate students who are seeking a scientific way of solving life problems and offering effective and efficient situations to the challenges facing our societies

Dr. Tawaziwa Wushe
Research Associate: University of South Africa
Doctor of Business Leadership
Master in Public Policy and Governance
Master of Business Administration
Chartered Management Consultant
Change Management Practitioner
Bachelor of Science Honours in Economics

DEDICATION

This book is dedicated to my only, late daughter, Faith Lucky.

PREFACE

This book tries to give a practical guideline to both master's and doctoral students on how to undertake their research project from inception to completion: from proposal to publication. It gives further guidance on how to approach the thesis defense and how to move one's thesis from an academic paper to a published piece in peer reviewed journals or turning the thesis to a book.

Students are expected to read other theoretical research books to supplement what can be learned from this short book. However, the book is expected to help students carry out their thesis writing more effectively and to be able to publish their thesis in the future.

CHAPTER 1

GENERAL GUIDELINES ON ACADEMIC RESEARCH

1.1 Introduction

Over the last ten years I have been involved in supervising MBA and PhD students in the African region in writing their theses and have also been involved as a member of many thesis defense panels. Through this experience, I have learnt the different challenges that students face in their thesis preparation and during the defense process. The majority of students face the same challenges because of similar factors which will be outlined in this book. Some of these challenges include working with academic supervisors, developing a strong research topic, writing the literature review and determining a conceptual framework and methodology for conducting research. Other problems include issues related to data analysis, report writing and thesis defense.

This book is will hopefully serve to open the eyes of students to the challenges they should expect in the process to write a thesis and help them overcome these issues so that they can create engaging and accurate theses and defend them effectively.

1.2 Book Objective

It is therefore my intention in this book to provide practical guidelines on how to approach the thesis process from the proposal preparation, to conducting research, preparing the research report and defending the research results. For each stage of the thesis preparation, I will try to explain theoretical as well as practical issues that students should understand and apply in order to create a quality thesis that is acceptable and further publishable in peer reviewed journals.

Students should not underestimate the amount of work required in creating a thesis and should not compare the process in any way to a simple course project. Thesis preparation requires a seriousness and much greater time commitment than any other academic project students face. In order for a student to produce a high-quality thesis, which is also publishable, I recommend that students take time to read research articles and journals and to familiarize themselves with the format and expectations of journal publishers. They should also try to access previous theses written by other students at their university through academic or online library searches.

1.3 Common Guidelines

Before discussing the detailed information required at each different stage of academic research, I would recommend the following order for an academic research report. This order is commonly accepted and promoted in most prestigious business schools around the world:

- Abstract
- Introduction
- Literature Review
- Conceptual Framework
- Research Methodology
- Research Findings
- Conclusions and Recommendations
- References
- Appendices

The following chapters will guide you through each of these stages with practical tips and strategies to complete them successfully. Using knowledge gained through teaching and supervising thesis students, I will also discuss weaknesses and challenges I have observed from my students in different African countries. Having supervised more than a hundred students in their thesis writing process from countries such as Tanzania, Kenya, Uganda, the Seychelles, Rwanda, Zambia, Zimbabwe, Malawi, Namibia, and Swaziland over the past twelve years, I am sure my suggestions and observations will be relevant to you in your thesis writing process.

1.4 Length of your Research Work

Thesis work requires extensive reading prior to and throughout the writing process. Outside readings will fit in every stage of your writing but are particularly important in the first chapter of your thesis. The length of the thesis will likely be set by the university for which you are writing the thesis. Different page number and word number minimums will be set by each university and without respecting these requirements, your work will not be accepted and may be disqualified.

1.5 Conclusion

This chapter has tried to introduce students to the objective of this book which is to provide practical guidelines on how to approach their thesis preparation from the proposal preparation, to conducting research and writing their research report to finally defending the research results. It has provided a standard outline or format which can be used to organize the thesis and it is one that most prestigious business schools teach and expect. However, students should remember that the proposed standard is only a guideline and other formats may better fit the students' research needs or may be required by their universities.

CHAPTER 2

WORKING WITH YOUR ACADEMIC SUPERVISOR

2.1 Introduction

First things first a student must understand that their supervisor has a full-time job with many responsibilities in addition to supervising them and, usually, several other students. Therefore, it is very important to follow the instructions given by one's supervisor so as not to waste their time or yours. It is not advisable for students to write to their supervisors daily or expect immediate communication back from their supervisor. Students who do not follow instructions tend to be the same students that write daily and expect immediate feedback from their supervisors. There should be a way of communicating with one's supervisor that creates a win-win situation for both parties which will result in less time wastage for all.

There are also cases of students who do not understand the role of the supervisor and essentially expect their supervisor to re-write their thesis instead rather than providing the support for the student to write their own thesis more effectively. Students, therefore, must understand that the role of the supervisor is simply to provide guidance to you on how to carry out your own research and what the expectations are for quality and quantity. Remember at the completion of your thesis work, the supervisor, at least at the master's level, is required to mark your work before you present it to your defense panel. Because of this, you should remember clearly that thesis writing is your responsibility and that you should not waste his or her time asking about every sentence or minor detail. This will come at the final revision stage just before your defense panel.

2.2   Getting the most from the supervisory relationship

The supervisor of your research will be the most important person for you as you write your thesis and will be the one who will help you create quality, reproduceable research. His or her contributions will support your efforts in the accomplishment of your research. Therefore, working and collaborating effectively with one's supervisor is critical for success. Students' should try to avoid any confrontation or behavior which may frustrate or demotivate their supervisor from assisting them in the timely completion of their thesis.

You should, therefore, focus on the following tips to make the most of the supervisory relationship:

a) ***Follow all supervisory instructions:*** This will help you complete your thesis on time without delay

b) ***Respond to all comments and feedback from your supervisor:*** When you stay quiet or delay implementing your supervisor's comments, you are the one who suffers—not your supervisor.

c) ***Stay humble:*** Remember that your supervisor is a professional who has already passed through his or her thesis stage and therefore likely knows much more than you. Never imply that you know better or refuse to change as this will create resentment and may reduce your supervisor's motivation to help you. I speak from experience as I once I had a student tell me point-blank that he would not change what he had written in his report. Upon hearing this, my interest in supporting him diminished as he had clearly closed the door to further improvement.

d) ***Seek mutual understanding:*** There may be times that you and your supervisor do not see eye to eye but avoid insisting that you know the only way. Find other professors or experts for additional support if needed but always act professionally.

2.3 Mind your Business: It is your work and not your supervisor's!

Many students who fail their thesis defense put the blame for their failure onto their supervisors, especially when their supervisors are not part of the defense. In one case I faced, a student who had not done his work to completion attempted to blame to his supervisor. However, we already knew the capability of the supervisor and his involvement with the student and so we ignored his entire claim: other students who passed their thesis were under the supervision of the same person!

In the end, students need to understand that the ultimate owner of the thesis is the student him or herself and so success or failure cannot be placed on one's supervisor. In rare cases supervisors may not have played their roles as effectively as needed but these are abnormal cases and should be brought to the attention of university administration early on in the process rather than after failing the defense. The role of a supervisor is to guide a student, critique the student's work and mark the work for approval for defense. Anything beyond this, is the full and complete responsibility of the student.

2.4 Dealing with challenges in the supervisory relationship

As already discussed above, supervisors play a major role in your thesis development. However, there are situations where a student may face serious challenges in the supervisory relationship for various reasons not limited to a lack of commitment from the supervisor or inadequate support given by the supervisor. In such cases, a student should report the matter as soon as possible to the university administrator over their immediate supervisor. Of course, this reporting should be limited to serious issues—minor differences of opinions or conflicts may arise, and these should be dealt with between the student and the supervisor.

Some challenges students' may face in their relationship with their thesis supervisor are as follows:

- a) ***No response to emails:*** The first action from a student in this challenge should be a polite reminder email or in-person reminder.

b) *Slow response time from supervisor*
c) *Unclear or Limited Explanation:* If information is unclear or too limited to be useful, a student should send a follow-up email requesting clarification to his or her supervisor.
d) *Abusive, demoralizing, or inappropriate remarks:* If a supervisor responds to a student in this way, the student may need to report the situation to a higher-level.
e) *Lack of knowledge of topic:* When a student recognizes that the supervisor, they have been given does not have the level of knowledge required to provide adequate support, he or she should report their concerns to the supervisor of their supervisor as this may impact their thesis success.
f) *Personal interest of the supervisor:* There are times when the supervisor wants you to concentrate on the topic which he or she has personal interest and you do not like the topic.

All these challenges and more others not mentioned here, should not discourage a student from completing their thesis. In all these challenges, a strategy to overcome the obstacle is needed so that the thesis process ends as a success.

2.5 Conclusion

This chapter has tried to explain basic issues that a student should consider in ensuring that he or she benefits as much as possible from the relationship with their thesis supervisor. One major takeaway from this chapter should be the understanding that the student is fully responsible for his or her success and so expecting one's supervisor to complete the thesis for you are shifting blame for failures onto one's supervisor are inappropriate actions.

Practice Questions

Question 1

Discuss how a student can create a useful and beneficial relationship with his or her thesis supervisor.

Question 2

How can a student deal with challenges in the supervisory relationship?

Questions 3

Discuss the reasons as to why students should take responsibility for the success of their theses.

CHAPTER 3
DEVELOPING THE RESEARCH TOPIC

3.1 Introduction

The research topic that a student chooses ultimately determines whether a student will finish their studies or not. Therefore, the choice of the topic is of crucial importance at the initial stage of any thesis study process. However, choosing a research topic might not be as easy as one thinks. Many topics you look into may have already been studied in depth, may lack literature support, may present data collection challenges, or the timeframe and passion required to research the topic exceptionally may not be there. Considering all of these issues early and completely before selecting a topic is vital for the success of the thesis research project long-term.

3.2 Formulating a Research Topic

Formulating a research topic is an art supported by in-depth study of the previous literature as well as empirical evidence from other scholars and the ability to define the current research problem. An individual can gather information that can help him or her to formulate a good research topic from different sources of information:

Magigi and Kazungu (2016) and Oso and Onen (2008) highlighted the most common sources of coming up research topic which include: Formal need assessments, personal experiences, deductions from existing theories and literature reviews. Personal experiences can be from previous research you have completed, and, in this case, you can identify gaps in your past research, or it can be from your personal experiences through observations, practices in the specific industry or involvement in previous studies. Formal assessment could involve need assessment for a specific problem in a country, society, or community etc. whereas literature reviews involve studying the literature from previous empirical studies and identifying areas which need more in-depth or specific research.

It is recommended that when you are formulating a research topic you should consider the following:

- ***Understandability:*** The reader should be able to quickly understand what you are researching based on your topic.
- ***Avoid ambiguity in topic selection:*** A clouded topic will try to cover too many topics in a single study. When a topic is clouded, you will not be able to formulate clear objectives, good research questions or an appropriate conceptual framework.
- ***Clear conceptual framework:*** A good topic is one which the reader /examiner recognizes the conceptual framework variables immediately. The two catch words that represent the conceptual framework are the independent and dependent variables. Using clear and succinct wording on a topic will keep these variables clear (We will talk more about this in the next few chapters!)

Table 1.1 below includes some examples of strong research topics which should help students understand how to develop an acceptable topic for research. In all five topics there is a clear topic definition with visible conceptual framework variables.

Table 1.1 Sample Selected Research Topic

S/No	Research Topic/Journal	Independent Variable	Dependent Variable
1	Financial sector reforms in bank ownership and its impact on service quality. Case of Commercial banks in Tanzania. **(Yona and Inanga, 2014)**	Financial Sector Reforms	Service Quality
2	The Impact of Professional Competence & Staffing of Internal Audit Function on Transparency and Accountability Case of Zimbabwe Local Authorities (**Jachi and Yona 2019**):	Professional Competence and Staffing	Transparency and Accountability
3	The Impact of Ethics & Objectivity of Internal Audit Personnel on Transparency & Accountability Case of Zimbabwe Local Authorities (**Jachi and Yona 2019**)	Ethics and Objectivity of Internal Audit Staff	Transparency and Accountability
4	The impact of Bank Ownership Structure on Bank Growth: Case of Tanzanian Commercial Banks. **Yona and Inanga (2016)**	Bank Ownership	Bank Growth
5	Bank ownership structure: Influence on Economic Efficiency of Commercial Banks; Case of Tanzanian Commercial Banks. **Yona and Inanga (2016)**	Bank Ownership Structure	Economic Efficiency

Source: Compiled Research Papers (2017-2019)

Consider the first topic, ***Financial Sector Reforms in Bank ownership and its impact on Service Quality.*** In this topic there is one independent variable: Financial sector reform on Bank Ownership; and one dependent variable: service quality.

In the second topic, ***The Impact of Professional Competence & Staffing of Internal Audit Function on Transparency and Accountability Case of Zimbabwe Local Authorities***, the independent variables are Professional competence and staffing while the dependent variables are transparency and accountability.

The third topic, ***The Impact of Ethics & Objectivity of Internal Audit Personnel on Transparency & Accountability Case of Zimbabwe Local Authorities***, also has two independent variables: Ethics and Objectivity of Internal Audit Personnel; and two dependent variables: transparency and accountability.

These examples have clearly stated topics which are not congested by too many words and their research variables are easily shown. The link between independent and dependent variable is recognizable at first glance. It is very important that the research topic should show the link of the variables at the outset so that the topic is not confusing to the reader.

In formulating a clear research topic, one should aim to have one major independent variable and one major dependent variable which can be operationalized in the conceptual framework chapter instead of showing all the variables in the topic which will make the topic to be too long and possibly confusing.

Consider the topic: ***The impact of Financial Sector Reforms on Banking Competitiveness"***: this is a very broad topic. Financial sector reforms are many and competitiveness is a very broad term. As far as a topic is concerned it may be fine, as it is clear that the independent variable is Financial Sector reforms and the dependent variable is Banking Competitiveness. However, in operationalizing the conceptual framework, one can come up with other independent variables related to financial sector reforms and others dependent variable's related to competitiveness. Putting all the variables into the main research topic will make it too long and confusing to readers.

3.3 Factors to consider before choosing a research topic

Before you choose a research topic, I would advise further consideration of the below-mentioned topics.

1. *Select a topic you are interested in:* Passion for a topic will help you put through the challenges of writing a thesis. This process is not easy and if you are researching a topic which you are not interested in, it becomes easier to quit when the going gets tough.
2. *Ensure research data is available for your topic:* Some topics are not researchable because data is too difficult to obtain because of confidentiality, national security, or other reasons.
3. *Consider the timeframe you have for your study:* Longitudinal studies and other long-term studies may not be possible to complete in the university time frame is which often only 6 months for master's level theses.
4. *Literature Availability is vital:* Don't reinvent the wheel but rather proceed where others have ended and focus on gaps in empirical research which have not yet but researched fully.
5. *Manage your language choices:* Avoid the use of vernacular or technical language which can confuse readers. Choose a short and simple topic title that can easily draw in a reader's attention.

3.4 Conclusion

Formulating a good research topic is key for successful thesis completion. A student who fails to formulate a strong research topic will find it difficult to see their thesis through to completion. This topic, therefore, helps students know how to formulate an effective research topic. The chapter has explained factors to consider when formulating and selecting a research topic.

Practice Questions

Question 1

Discuss the challenges in developing an idea into a research topic.

Question 2

What factors should be considered before selecting a research topic?

Question 3

What are the qualities of a strong research topic?

CHAPTER 4
ORGANIZING THE INTRODUCTION CHAPTER

4.1 Introduction

This chapter is designed to help students to formulate the historical background to support a research problem, formulate the research problem, state the research objectives and develop research questions. In this same chapter, readers will learn to show the significance of their research, define research scope and identify possible limitations to the study. At the end of this chapter, one should have a clear picture of how research should be organized. The first chapter of your thesis lays out the background information for your research. It is expected that chapter one should be organized with specific sections in this format:

1.1. Introduction
1.2. Background of the Country/Company /Sector/Region /Department
1.3. Purpose of the study
1.4. Statement of the research problem
1.5. Research objectives
1.6. Research questions
1.7. Significance of the research
1.8. Research scope and limitations
1.9. Organization of the thesis

It is the intention of this chapter to explain, in brief, what is expected in each of these sections. The explanation may not be conclusive, but it should become clearer what the key issues that should be included in explanations.

4.2 Writing the Historical Background of the Research

Before writing the historical background to the research, one should understand that research is an in-depth investigation of a subject matter in order to discover the cause of the problem. It is about searching for the truth about a problem in order to establish the cause and providing a solution to the problem. Therefore, it will require a student to perform an in-depth investigation into the subject matter before making any conclusions or recommendations about the subject matter.

Before defining the research problem, stating research objectives or creating research questions, students need to establish the historical background of the research subject matter. It is very important that as a researcher one has enough quality information about the topic before endeavoring to research it. This requires the student to go through different literature and reports and gather statistics as necessary to have a clear picture of what is behind the subject. Writing a historical background requires one to select specific information that can help in understanding the background of the country in which the research is to be carried out and possibly the background of the industry, area, sector or company related to the research topic.

4.3 Purpose of the study

In this section a student needs to be clear on their reasons for studying the specific subject matter. The purpose should be stated in simple language that any reader can understand the reasons for undertaking such a study. What the researcher hopes to achieve from the study should also be clear. The following example from a study titled, *"The impact of Bank ownership on banking competitiveness: Case of Commercial Banks in Tanzania"* provides a clear purpose of study:

"The purpose of the study is to determine the effect of bank ownership (semi-quasi and private banks) on banking competitiveness as measured by service quality, growth, profitability, financial soundness and efficiency of commercial banks in Tanzania" (Yona 2016).

4.4 Defining the Research Problem

Defining the research problem is the essence of all academic research work. Poor definition of one's research problem leads to inability to articulate the research objectives and poor formulation of research questions. Understanding any problem that needs to be investigated or studied is the key success factor for research. Understanding what needs to be studied also helps the researcher to clearly define the problem in a simple way which, at the end, makes it easier to investigate a subject matter to the depth expected for a thesis.

A question one may ask him or herself is, "How can I understand that there is a problem that needs to be studied? The answer to this question is not simple. It should include all of the below:

1. ***Studying the previous research work done by other academic scholars*** on the subject matter. This should give you an idea of past problems already identified in this subject matter and hence establish the gaps that need further studying. Studying the previous empirical literature can help a researcher to discover an investigated problem, the data collection method, and the analysis process utilized in prior investigations too.

    In each paper you read you will be able to identify gaps which were not addressed by the previous studies and could serve as your investigation point. At the same time, by reading previous academic papers, you will also discover problems which now look similar to the problems in the present industry and sector that you want to study. It is not illegal to repeat studies done elsewhere as long as you acknowledge those studies and how they differ from you study (i.e. different sample size or different methodology). It is important that you give a justification for repeated studies.

2. ***Observe what is happening in the business environment, industry or sector you are studying and be able to identify the problem during the observation time.*** Taking this further we can say that observation involves spending time in observing what has physically happened, why is it happening, how things are done. Possibly from this point someone is capable of identifying what the problem is and what may have been done incorrectly.

4.5 Stating the Research Objectives

After defining the research problem clearly, what follows is to state the research objectives. When conducting academic research, one should have a clear objective to achieve by the end of the research. Alexander (2008) emphasizes that a research objective should be clearly defined and measurable at the end.

The research objective can be clearly defined as the primary reason for conducting the research. The objective of one's research will vary depending on the type of the research undertaken. Research objectives are expected to establish the root cause of the research problem articulated in the statement of the problem. When stating the research problem, it should be stated in simple language so that all readers can understand it.

It is recommended to state the main research objective first followed by the specific research objectives. When stating the main research objective, one should ensure it is in harmony with the topic and should not be too ambiguous.

Major and specific research objectives should also be in harmony with the independent and dependent variables of the conceptual framework. There should be agreement between the specific research objectives and the variables stated as independent or dependent variables. Lack of homogeneity will make it the study more difficult to conduct. Clear, specific objectives that are straight-forward should help make clarity around independent and dependent variables.

Consider the following example of a research topic titled, "**The Impact of Bank Ownership on Banking Competitiveness**" (Yona, 2016). In this case, the main research objective is stated as: *'To establish the influence of bank ownership structure on the banking competitiveness of commercial banks in Tanzania'.*

Specific research objectives were stated hereunder:

1. *To determine whether bank ownership structure affects service quality of Tanzanian Commercial banks;*
2. *To assess the extent to which bank ownership structure influences the growth of commercial banks;*
3. *To find out whether bank ownership structure influences the financial soundness of Tanzanian commercial banks*
4. *To determine the extent to which bank ownership structure influences efficiency of Tanzanian commercial banks*

From the above one should note the following issues:

- The main research objective is in harmony with the research topic:
- Each specific objective (SPO) has both an independent and a dependent variable. One can clearly see these variables without much difficulty and can easily determine what is going to be studied.

SPO1:
    Independent variable: bank ownership structure.
    Dependent variable: service quality

SPO2:
    Independent variable: bank ownership structure
    Dependent variable: growth of commercial banks

SPO3:
    Independent variable: bank ownership structure
    Dependent variable: financial soundness

SPO 4:
>*Independent Variable:* bank ownership
>*Dependent Variable*: efficiency

One thing which is important in your study, because of time limitations, in order to complete the study on time is good to avoid too many specific objectives in one study. If there are too many specific objectives, the time available by the student might not be adequate enough to complete the study. It is recommended that for master's degree studies should not have more than three specific objectives to allow the researcher to complete the work in a shorter period of time.

4.6   Designing the Research Questions

Stating research questions is not difficult to do especially when the research objectives are clearly defined and are in harmony with the conceptual framework. The research questions should be made on the basis of the research objectives. The intention of a researcher should be that all answers to research questions should provide solutions to the research problem. Blaxter et al. (2006) emphasize that research questions should not be too long but rather narrow, clear and well-defined. Furthermore, all research questions should be appropriate to the topic and research objectives. It is important to have one main research question and specific questions which originate from the specific research objectives.

Consider the following example of a main research topic titled, "***The Impact of Bank Ownership on Banking Competitiveness (Yona, 2016).*** In this case the main research questions were formed by re-framing the main research objectives into the form of a question:

"What *is the impact of bank ownership on banking competitiveness?*" Research questions should always end with a question mark.

Specific research questions of this study are the re-framed research objectives stated above under section 4.5 which were modified to create the following specific research questions:

1. To what extent does bank ownership structure affect the service quality of Tanzanian commercial banks?

2. To what extent does bank ownership structure affect the growth of the Tanzanian commercial banks?
3. To what extent does bank ownership structure affect profitability and financial soundness of Tanzanian commercial banks?
4. To what extent does bank ownership structure affect the efficiency of Tanzanian commercial banks?

One should also note that in designing research questions, you cannot have more research questions than research objectives. In other words, the number of research questions should be equal to the number of research objectives.

4.7 Significance of the Research

In this section the student is expected to explain the importance of their research and who will likely benefit from the research findings. It is in this section where justification of the research should be done. The student should articulate in clear language, the benefits of the study. The student is expected to demonstrate that the study findings will add value to the body of knowledge. Furthermore, the student is expected to show how the thesis will benefit other stakeholders such as the government policymakers and industry practitioners. Below in Box 1 is an example of the significance of the study in a study titled **"The Impact of Bank Ownership on banking competitiveness: Case of Commercial Banks in Tanzania"**.

Box 1: Example of the Significance of the Research

> The study is of significant importance to the government of Tanzania as well as to commercial banks. Through this study, banks will be able to understand their current competitive status, areas of improvement that support the enhancement of service quality dimensions, bank growth, efficiency, financial soundness and profitability in order to enhance future competitiveness.
>
> The use of the research findings from this study will benefit government officials in their consideration of other possible policies that are likely to influence banking competitiveness beyond reforms on banking ownership.
>
> Moreover, the study will add value to the body of knowledge in the discourse of financial sector reforms and banking competitiveness. With this body of knowledge, the government of Tanzania policymakers will appreciate the role which bank ownership structure play in influencing service quality, bank growth, financial soundness, profitability and efficiency of the commercial banks. In addition to the knowledge on bank ownership structure on banking competitiveness, the study will reveal if there are other factors likely to have impact on bank competitiveness. The body of knowledge will address the gap of empirical evidences lacking to address such important issues in the context of developing countries like Tanzania.
>
> Source: Yona (2016)

4.8 Research Scope and Limitations

In all research activities, the researcher should clearly state how far he or she will conduct the research activities. In other words, one should state if the study is a country study, regional, district, case study or single company study. One should clearly state what will be studied and what will not be studied with proper justification of these decisions and should recognize that you cannot study everything at one time because of time and resource considerations.

In the study of, *"The Impact of Financial Sector Reforms on Banking Competitiveness in Tanzania"* (Yona 2016), the scope was limited to financial sector reforms related to bank ownership and its impact on banking competitiveness. There were many reforms that the government of Tanzania undertook in 2000 including interest rates liberalization and liberalization of foreign exchange controls. The temptation to try to study all of these issues at the same time was there but the scope made the study focus only on bank ownership-- even competitiveness was scaled down to study only a few measurements of competitiveness. Studying everything related to bank ownership and competitiveness would make the study never-ending.

In this same section, a student should state what likely limitations there may be. The majority of students prefer to use a common statement that finance and time are the limitations of their study, but these are not the only limitations that studies face. There are multiple issues that are likely to impair research work. However, students should be specific and clearly mention limitations of their studies rather than beating around the bush. Limitations will vary from one study to another, from one country to another and so on. The limitations include all constraints that are likely to impair research activities such as inadequate data or lack of experience in using certain types of quantitative analysis techniques as well as any other factors that might hinder the research work.

In his book, 'The Ultimate Guide to Writing a Dissertation in Business Studies: A Step-by-Step Assistance', John (2018) argues that someone can formulate research aims and objectives too broadly such that they become a limitation, or someone having no extensive experience in primary data collection which can lead the implementation of data collection method to be flawed (2018). One should explicitly state the true limitations of the study rather than copying statements from previous studies.

As each study is unique, defining the boundaries of one's research will help them focus on specific issues, sectors, or locations. The definition of the scope of the research now becomes important. The research scope defines the parameters of the research-- how far should you go with the study. The parameters might include the country of study, the industry, kind of data you expect to use in your research, the study population, data collection methods and techniques.

Reviewing the following example in Box 2 of research scope and limitation in the study titled, **"The Impact of Bank Ownership on Banking Competitiveness: Case of Commercial Banks in Tanzania"** may help bring this information from theoretical to practical in the minds of readers.

Box 2: Example of Research Scope and Limitation

The study was limited to financial sector reforms in the bank ownership structure and its influence on banking competitiveness as measured by service quality, banking efficiency, bank growth, profitability and financial soundness of the commercial banks in Tanzania.

There are many areas of reforms that Tanzania undertook from the year 2000 such as liberalisation of interest rates and the liberalisation of foreign exchange control, but the study was limited to only one area of the financial sector reforms namely bank ownership. The study was also limited in the sense that it concentrated on the examination of the commercial banks in Tanzania. It excluded the micro-finance institutions, investment banks and the central bank that also provides banking services which could have been influenced by the financial sector reforms.

The research adopted a descriptive study method for only thirty-two commercial banks in Tanzania that were registered with the Bank of Tanzania by the end of year 2011.

4.9 Organization of Your Research

The organization of your research should be the last thing included in chapter one of a thesis. This section should explain how you are going to organize your research work by providing a clear map of how the chapters of a thesis will come together. Information will be included about how many chapters will thesis contain and what is expected in each written chapter. This section does not require extreme detail and it should be no more than one page.

Consider the following example on how to organize a thesis adapted from a previous PhD thesis:

Box 3: Example - Organization of Research Work

> "This research paper comprises of six chapters, including this chapter. The following are the chapters that are included in this thesis. Chapter one discusses the historical background to the research problem, a statement of the problem, research objectives, and research questions, the significance of the research as well as research scope and limitations. Chapter two (Literature Review) will discuss the background of the financial Sector in Tanzania as well as highlight the reforms carried at over the period of the study as well as to their objectives. It will further discuss the key issues on financial sector reforms, theories on reforms, findings of other studies as well as competitiveness in the context of the banking industry and the experiences of other countries on financial sector reforms. Chapter 3 (Research Methodology) will present the methods and procedures used to collect and analyze the data for this study. Chapter 4 describes the major findings for each of the research questions. Lastly, chapter five gives the summary of each chapter of the research and recommendations for further research."
>
> Source: Yona (2016)

4.10 Research Coherence

Research coherence is an important aspect of any research design. However, there is no assigned portion of chapter one dedicated just to research coherence. It should rather be seen in throughout all chapters of the thesis -- meaning that there should be cohesion between all areas of the research study throughout the thesis. There should be harmony between the discussions of historical background, statement of the problem, research objectives and research questions.

Chenail et al. (2011) indicate that coherence means the existence of a correlation between the topic, statement of problem and research objectives. Furthermore, coherence is evidenced by the existence of a clear study focus and the literature discussion as well as an interconnectedness between the literature review and research questions.

At the end of a research study, the evaluators will review the study's overall cohesion. There is weak study coherence where:

a. Your research topic is not in harmony with the statement of the problem and research objectives;
b. The research objectives are not in harmony with the research questions;
c. The conceptual framework is not in harmony with research objectives and research questions;
d. The abstract section is disconnected from the statement of the problem, research objectives, research questions, methodology and research findings;
e. There are unrelated correlations between research findings and research questions. This means that the research findings are providing answers which do not relate with the research questions and hypotheses of the study.
f. Research instruments used are inappropriate for the research objectives.
g. Research methodology is inadequate for the research findings.

Therefore, it is very important for a student to review his or her work on continuous basis to ensure overall cohesion. Absence of cohesiveness in one's thesis waters down the quality of the research. The cohesion should be observed from the initial stages of your research work through to the end.

4.11 Conclusions

The chapter's aim was to explain basic steps in developing the introduction chapter of one's thesis. The chapter gave details for students to better understand how to formulate a problem statement, give justification to their research and formulate research objectives and research questions.

The chapter has also explained how students can come up with statements on the significance of the study and explain the scope and limitations of the study.

Chapter One of a thesis is not expected to have a section on research coherence as previously mentioned. However, the chapter has tried to explain what research cohesion is and why it is important for students to understand this concept from the beginning so that they don't create inconsistencies in their research work.

Practice Questions

Question 1

Discuss the characteristics of a great research topic.

Question 2

What are the main resources an individual can use to gather necessary information to formulate a good research topic? Discuss each method mentioned.

Question 3

Discuss the qualities of an effective research objective. Why is it important to have main research objective and specific research objectives?

Question 4

What is the difference between the purpose and significance of a study? Explain.

Question 5

What should be discussed in regard to the scope and limitations of one's research?

CHAPTER 5

ORGANIZING THE LITERATURE REVIEW

5.1 Introduction

The literature review chapter is an important part of your research thesis. The chapter should include an introduction to the chapter, discussion of key research variables, theoretical discussion of the research conducted, empirical discussions and links between the current and previously completed studies. The introduction section of the literature review is not expected to be too long but rather a brief snapshot of the chapter contents.

It is important that a student understands that the literature review is a piece of academic work that requires in-depth study of previous and existing literature on the subject matter to be researched and of the theories related to the study. The review of related literature should open the eyes of the student to exactly what needs to be studied so as to avoid duplication or repetition of similar studies undertaken by other scholars. One may find it useful to focus on gaps in prior studies as these create a platform for new studies.

5.2 Elements of a Research Literature Review

A literature review is a detailed study of existing writings and theories relating to the subject matter you intend to study and how those theories can be applied to one's current study. Literature review also involves the study of previous literature about the topic including theories, research and other related information. Aveyard (2010) defines a literature review as an in-depth study and interpretation of key issues related to specific topic. To conduct an effective literature review, one must utilize a systematic search, critique and combine of various literature studies, and recognize gaps in the literature which may be appropriate entry points for new research.

The literature review provides initial understanding and knowledge of the topic to the new researcher and helps him or her understand if other researchers have already studied the subject. It clarifies whether further research around a topic is even needed and provides a way to give credit to previous scholars.

Proper Literature review will follow a sequence of events as outlined in Table 5.1 below.

Table 5.1 Elements of Literature Review

1. Identify empirical works in the study and ascertain the researcher worked on the topic you are studying
2. Get clarification of ideas, conclusions and theories and establish similarities & differences
3. Determine the research techniques and methodologies used and their major findings
4. Identify research gaps
5. Formalize relationships between previous studies or theories
6. Provide context for your own research
7. Explore existing information in the fields of research

Source: https://www.lib.ncsu.edu/tutorials/litreview/

5.3   Expectations for a Thesis Literature Review

A literature review involves a critical review of what has been written about the subject matter by previous scholars. It involves also reviewing of the theories adopted by previous studies with a critique of them and clearly stated linkage between prior studies and one's specific study. In order to have a robust literature review, the central research question should guide the review. Students should avoid writing a literature review which strays from the key issues related to the study at hand. A proper literature review should include an adequate number of studies so that the review is not seen as shallow. It is also very important to select up-to-date, relevant literature.

A thesis literature review lays down the foundation of understanding what is being studied. It will explore in detail the knowledge behind the subject matter and reveal if there were any previous investigations of the subject prior to one's current study. The literature review should reveal the findings of the previous studies and show what gaps were not addressed and how those gaps will be addressed in the current study.

Conducting a literature review does not mean one writes everything they know about the topic but is instead limited to the study of specific parameters. It must involve an extensive study of the existing literature on the subject matter to be investigated and should include current and past theories as well as how these theories are linked to the current study of choice.

The student should also consider the scope of his or her study review in regard to how many studies should be reviewed and the date range of the studies to be selected. While specific rules about quoting literature and citing it in your paper will depend on your university's stylistic requirements (i.e. Harvard style, APA, MPA), all students should commit to one citation style and should only use up-to-date and relevant literature in their literature review.

5.4 Avoiding Plagiarism

A pitfall which can destroy the legitimacy of an individual's literature review is plagiarism when it comes to citation of references. Plagiarism in writing the literature review and, in reality, the thesis as a whole, is unacceptable. This is a critical issue to hash out as many students don't even know what plagiarism is. Plagiarism is basically using someone else's work without giving them credit.

Plagiarism involves copying, paraphrasing, not putting a quotation, giving wrong quotations, or adopting another person's work without acknowledgement of that person. Actually, plagiarism is considered as theft of another person work. To avoid plagiarism, students need to know how to read another person's work and when it comes to citations, knowing how to acknowledge that work can prevent plagiarism. Writing is considered plagiarism when one uses another person's writings without acknowledging the person who wrote the piece and presents the work as their own without acknowledging the person who actually wrote it. This goes hand in hand also with all quotations without including the quotation marks (',') at the beginning or end of the sentences.

Furthermore, when an individual misrepresents the source of the information, this is also plagiarism. It can be through copying sentences from a text and using them in your writing without acknowledging the original author. The best way to avoid all this is to know how to properly cite any source of information you use as plagiarism can lead to expulsion from a graduate program of student and/or rejection of one's thesis.

In modern times students can avoid plagiarism by using software to check their work if there is any element of plagiarism which they might have missed. Software is available online for free or for reasonable and affordable prices which are worthwhile for helping students' check their work. Examples of these software programs include the Plagscan, Quetext, Grammarly.com Plagiarism checker and many others which can be found through a simple google search. Students may want to explore several different types of plagiarism software to find one which they are comfortable with for their thesis but the importance of checking for plagiarism in one way or another cannot be overstated.

5.5 Standard Citation Formats and Requirements

As already mentioned above, writing literature review requires students to adopt a certain style of making citation from the literature reviewed. Each university will require you to follow a certain citation style and you need to comply. Example of international citation standards include the Harvard style, APA Style, Turabian Style, and many others.

Table 5.1 below shows how you can use the APA style to gives citation in your research work. The table shows citations to use when citing a book by a single author, multiple authors or a book editor. It further shows how to cite journal articles when there is a single author or multiple authors. Finally, the standard also shows how to cite a thesis or dissertation and any non-periodical web document in the website. Reading and frequently reviewing the table below will assist students in understanding and accurately citing work from a variety of sources so as to prevent any unintentional plagiarism.

Table 5.2 APA Citation Format

Book, Single Author	Ball, P. (2001). *Bright earth: Art and the invention of color.* New York: Farrar, Straus and Giroux.
Book, Multiple Authors	Bird, K., & Martin, J. S. (2005). *American Prometheus: The triumph and tragedy of J. Robert Oppenheimer.* New York: Alfred A. Knopf.
Book, Editor	Silverstein, T. (Ed). (1974). *Sir Gawain and the green knight.* Chicago: University of Chicago Press.
Chapter in a Book	Demos, J. (2001). Real lives and other fictions: Reconsidering Wallace Stegner's *Angle of Repose*. In Carnes, M. (Ed.), *Novel history: Historians and novelists confront America's past (and each other)*, (pp. 132-145). New York: Simon and Schuster.
Journal Article	Burns, S. (2005). Ordering the artist's body: Thomas Eakins' acts of self-portrayal. *American Art, 19*(1), 90-102.
Journal Article with DOI	Murdock, L., & Hobbs, J. (2011, July). Picture me playing: Increasing pretend play dialogue of children with autism spectrum disorders. *Journal of Autism and Developmental Disorders, 41*(7), 870-878. doi: 10.1007/s10803-010-1108-6
Journal Article without a DOI	Tilak, J.G. (2002). Education and poverty. *Journal of Human Development, 3*(2)191-207.Retrieved from http://www.tandfonline.com/loi/cjhd20
Thesis or Dissertation	Erickson, C. (2008). *Critical multiculturalism and preservice teacher education* (Doctoral dissertation, University of West Florida Website (non-periodical web document) Florida Department of Education. (2010). *Next generation sunshine state standards: Grade two, social studies.* Retrieved from http://www.floridastandards.org/Standards/FLStandardSearch.aspx Source: *Publication Manual of the American Psychological Association (2010) 6th Edition*). Retrieved from *http://purl.fcla.edu/fcla/etd/WFE000011*

Source: Publication Manual of the American Psychological Association (2010) 6th Edition

Turbian citation standards are different from APA citation standards. The decision to use a particular citation style may be personal or, as per usual, depends on the requirements of the university. Table 5.2 below shows how you can do citations when citing a book by one single author, multiple authors or a book editor in this citation format. It further shows how to cite journal articles when there is a single author or multiple authors. Finally, the standard also shows how to cite a thesis or dissertation as well as when citing any non-periodical web document in the website.

Table 5.3 Turbian Citation

Book, Single Author 14.18	N	1. Michael Pollan, *The Omnivore's Dilemma: A Natural History of Four Meals* (New York: Penguin, 2006), 99-100.
	B	Pollan, Michael. *The Omnivore's Dilemma: A Natural History of Four Meals*. New York: Penguin, 2006.
Book, Multiple Authors 14.18	N	2. Geoffrey C. Ward and Ken Burns, *The War: An Intimate History, 1941-1945* (New York: Knopf, 2007), 52.
	B	Ward, Geoffrey C., and Ken Burns. *The War: An Intimate History, 1941-1945*. New York: Knopf, 2007.
Book, Editor or Translator 14.18	N	3. Joel Greenberg, ed., *Of Prairie, Woods, and Water: Two Centuries of Chicago Nature Writing* (Chicago: University of Chicago Press, 2008), 42.
	B	Greenberg, Joel, ed. *Of Prairie, Woods, and Water: Two Centuries of Chicago Nature Writing*. Chicago: University of Chicago Press, 2008.
Book, Editor or Translator in Addition to Author 14.18	N	4. Gabriel Garcia Marquez, *Love in the Time of Cholera*, trans. Edith Grossman (London: Cape, 1988), 242-55.
	B	Garcia Marquez, Gabriel. *Love in the Time of Cholera*. Translated by Edith Grossman. London: Cape, 1988.
Chapter in an Edited Book 14.18	N	5. Glenn Gould, "Streisand as Schwarzkopf," in *The Glenn Gould Reader*, ed. Tim Page (New York: Vintage, 1984), 310.
	B	Gould, Glenn. "Streisand as Schwarzkopf." In *The Glenn Gould Reader*, edited by Tim Page, 308-11. New York: Vintage, 1984.
Book, Later Edition 14.118	N	6. Karen V. Harper-Dorton and Martin Herbert, *Working with Children, Adolescents, and Their Families*, 3rd ed. (Chicago: Lyceum Books, 2002), 43.
	B	Harper-Dorton, Karen V., and Martin Herbert. *Working with Children, Adolescents, and Their Families*. 3rd ed. Chicago: Lyceum Books, 2002.

Source: Chicago Manual (Turbian Citation) 17th Edition

Harvard citation format, often required by business schools, differs as well from APA and Turbian standards. The decision to use style also depends on the requirements of the university too. The table (Table 5.3) below shows how you can do citations when citing a book by one single author and multiple authors. It further shows how to cite journal articles when there is a single author or multiple authors. Finally, the standard also shows how to cite a thesis or dissertation as well as when citing any non-periodical web document in the website.

Table 5.4 Harvard Citation Format

Book with one Author	Tim, H (1997) Mastering Statistics. 3rd Edition, MacMillan
Book with two authors or three	Gail, P, Dennis, F, Lenore, S (2018). Heads of Mission, A Handbook. Xlibris
Book with four Authors	James, P., Croft, D., Levin, S. and Doe, A. (1998). How to Succeed in the Restaurant Industry. Nottingham: Delectable Publications.
Journal Article	Yona, L. (2016).
Citations for Journal Articles accessed on a website or database	Jenkins, O. (1996). Unusual Recipes and Cantonese Cuisine. Culinary Research, Volume 5 (8), pp. 47-59. Available at: www.culinaryresearchjournal.com/jenkinsocanteonese

Source: Authors Compilation (2020)

5.6   Organizing your Literature Review

In addition to maintaining a strong grasp of citation formatting, students must also focus on the organization of their literature review. Work should be organized to create a clear flow of information for any and all readers to understand the research basics.

Literature reviews should be written in proper order and should maintain a clear arrangement of subtopics and sections-- not written as a fiction story. Each subtopic and section discussion should have adequate and appropriate literature to support. Students should avoid writing long paragraphs in any section without external literature support. Where possible, a paragraph should be no more than ten and no less than two sentences. Remember that a literature review is not storytelling but is rather about the analysis of issues, arguments and relevant facts. Academic, formal language should always be adhered to in the literature review, and in fact, throughout the entire thesis.

5.7 Theoretical Review

In the theoretical review section, students are expected to discuss relevant, prevailing theories on the subject matter which they are researching. The discussion should include background on the origin of the theories discussed, their key postulates and how the theories are linked to previous similar studies. Students are also expected to give reasons or justification for including each specific theory in their study and, if possible, should explain any links between those studies and the students' own research.

Some study topics have numerous theories discussed in relevant literature. Students who find this situation may be tempted to discuss too many theories which are not linked at all or are distantly linked to their research. Students should only select theories with a clear relationship to the current study. When one theory is derived from another theory, students should explain why they focused on one or the other and should outline the relationship between these theories.

5.8 Empirical Literature

In this section, students are expected to show, explain and discuss the previous studies on the subject matter. The empirical literature provides insights of understanding the current study by examining previous studies by different scholars. The empirical literature will underscore previous findings on the subject matter. It shows various studies which have been done on the subject matter.

Empirical literature are previously verified studies on the topic understudy on which one lays the foundation of the current study rather than re-inventing the wheel. It helps to show the expected relationship or correlation between the previous studies and current study.

The proper way of writing the empirical literature is to use different writing style: It should not be written as a story telling of what happened in the past only. It is expected that, In any empirical literature review we expect to know in each article or journal reviewed for example: proper citation of name the researcher, the year of research, research methodology used to arrive at the findings which could also include the total sample used, major findings and study conclusions. The researcher can also give a critical review on the methodology and findings and give his or his own observations of the gaps from the previous studies examined.

However, not all literature is considered to be empirical literature. The following sources of information do not meet the standards to qualify as empirical literature: textbooks, political statements, Facebook or Instagram information, blog postings, advertisements, newspapers and magazines or Television news reports.

5.9 Common mistakes in writing a Literature Review

Since we have learned a lot about what to do in a literature review, now is the appropriate time to also mention what we should not do. There are a number of common mistakes that students make in completing their literature reviews which are outlined below to try to prevent readers of this book from doing the same. Many students make these common mistakes:

- *Using informal language in one's literature review:* A literature review is not a story or a letter—it is a formal academic writing piece and therefore should be formatted that way.
- ***Not adhering to the rules of proper academic citation:*** It is not acceptable to write long paragraphs without any citations though it is quite common to find students do just that.
- *Using personalized titles:* If you are writing about someone whose last name is Said, you must refer to him as Said rather than Mr. Said.
- ***Paragraphs that are too short or too long:*** Paragraphs should be between two and ten sentences in length—no more, no less.
- *Using outdated resources:* In this day and age, resources are in absolute abundance. There is no reason to include references which are more than just a few years old except when presenting a history of theories. All journal articles and research samples should be recent.
- ***Lack of attention to format details:*** Students must adhere to the requirements set out for them in regard to font type and size. From the first page to the last page of the thesis document, the font size and type should be consistent.

- ***Poor organization of ideas:*** Ideas must be organized into paragraphs, sections and sub-sections. These sections should be correctly numbers for the ease of the reader.
- ***Clouded literature selections:*** As a thesis supervisor myself I have found that many students attempt to discuss everything they can find about a topic without actually showing a true understanding of the information and without clearly linking the information to their current research. Every word should be linked to your research objectives and conceptual framework.
- ***Including photographs or illustrations:*** Photographs and illustrations are only permissible as part of appendices, not part of the literature review. Tables are also not recommended in this section.
- ***Shallow discussion of literature or inadequate literature in general:*** Students must keep in mind the word count and page requirements set out by their university and should use them the best way possible. Discussion should be well thought-out and presented professionally. It should be obvious to the evaluator that the student spent time and mental effort developing the literature review.

5.10 Sources of Literature

Literature reviews require extensive scholarly review of various literature from different sources. Where you gather the information and the type of information it matters a lot in any research work. Literature review can be generated from primary source or secondary source.

> **Primary source:** considered to be firsthand information that is the closest to the object of the study. Galvan (2013) explains that in social science, original reports from academic journals, in-depth descriptions and discussions of the findings are considered as primary sources of information. Primary source is also termed as empirical literature or empirical evidences.
>
> Parsaud (2018) considers speeches, letters, interviews, official reports, conference proceedings, company reports

and unpolished manuscripts as primary sources. Primary sources for literature review are characterized by a higher level of details and little time needed to publish (John 2018).

Secondary Sources: According to Galvan (2013) secondary sources provide secondhand information or data which are not created by the author. They are not original or new sources. Secondary sources can include newspapers, textbooks, magazines and biographies. Secondary sources for literature reviews are characterized by a medium level of detail and medium time needed to publish.

Tertiary Sources: Mary (2020) defines tertiary sources as those which are used to organize and locate secondary and primary sources. Example of tertiary source include indexes, abstracts and databases.

Apart from understanding various types of sources for literature reviews, in academic research, some information should be avoided when writing your literature review chapter such as sources which are not evidence or research based as these tend to lower the quality of the literature review. Literature sources are not expected to be fictional information or stories but rather should be empirical information supported by data from previous reputable studies.

5.11 Conclusion

This chapter should provide readers with clear guidelines about how to organize their thesis literature review chapter effectively.This chapter has explained the key elements of a literature review, expectations for the contents of the literature review, how to avoid plagiarism and standard citations requirements as well as addressing some of the most common mistakes in creating a literature review.

Practice Questions

Question 1

What are the qualities of a strong literature review for any research paper?

Question 2

What are some common mistakes made when writing a literature review?

Question 3

What is the difference between a theoretical review and an empirical review?

Question 4

Explain the differences between APA, Harvard and Turbian citation formatting?

CHAPTER 6
CONCEPTUAL FRAMEWORK

6.1 Introduction

There have been evolving practices in the proper placement of one's conceptual framework in their thesis preparation. Traditionally the conceptual framework has been included as a part of the literature review chapter—always added to the end of that chapter. However, recent developments in academic research show a shift whereas many universities are now requiring students to consider the conceptual framework as a separate chapter to follow the literature review. Other universities have suggested that the conceptual framework should be part of a combined conceptual framework and research methodology chapter. In this case, the conceptual framework will be discussed first and then the research methodology will follow. The placement of the conceptual framework discussion in a student's thesis will be determined by the requirements of the university or business school at which they are studying.

When reading past theses, students may feel confused with these organizational differences. However, what is important is that the students stick to their program's guidelines and, wherever it is placed, students must understand what should be included in this important thesis section.

6.2   What is a Conceptual Framework?

The conceptual framework lays out the key issues that the study will engage. It provides the road map of what should be studied, and it gives the boundaries on what one should not study. It gives clear parameters of the study and how each parameter is linked to the others. The conceptual framework determines the independent and dependent variables and, in some studies, might also set out moderating and intervening variables. Students with a short time frame should focus on studies with independent and dependent variables only.

Drawing the Conceptual Framework

The conceptual framework should be directional. It has to give proper direction by showing the independent variable, moderating variables, intervening variables and the dependent variables. While not all studies include all the mentioned variables, in most cases, to avoid a clouded conceptual framework, it makes sense to show your variables in a flow chart diagram. The independent variables should start first and should show its linkage to the dependent variable. Figure 6.1 below is a very simple diagram of a conceptual framework adapted from a research topic "The impact of Bank ownership on banking Competitiveness" (Yona 2016), which shows bank ownership structure as an independent variable and Bank Competitiveness as a dependent variable. Using a diagram such as this will help one formulate appropriate related research objectives and questions. It is very important to draw arrows which are directional, or which shows which variable is influenced and which variables influence other variables. The diagram below shows that it is the independent variable (Bank ownership) which is influencing the dependent variable (Banking Competitiveness) and not vice versa. This example is the simplest conceptual framework with only independent and dependent variable. Where there are other variables such as moderating and intervening variable you have to include them in the flow chart showing how they influence the dependent variables. One thing one should remember is that all the variables depicted in the conceptual framework they should be related to the study, they should be defined and explained with support of the literature. The variables in the conceptual framework are key issues that support the formulation of the research objectives and research questions.

Figure 6.1 Conceptual framework

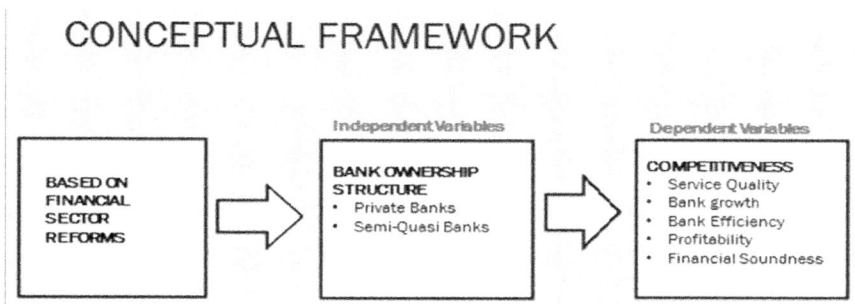

Source: Yona (2016): The Impact of Bank Ownership on Banking Competitiveness

The above conceptual framework in Figure 6.1 which shows only two variables namely the independent and dependent variables. From this conceptual framework, one can easily see the linkage between these variables and formulate research questions based on the relationship between these variables as follows:

i. To evaluate the extent to which extent bank ownership structure influences the service quality of commercial banks in Tanzania
ii. To examine the influence of bank ownership structure growth of commercial banks in Tanzania
iii. To evaluate the extent to which bank ownership structure influences the financial soundness of commercial banks in Tanzania

These research objectives can be translated easily into key specific research questions

i. To what extent bank ownership structure influences the service quality of commercial banks in Tanzania?
ii. To what extent bank ownership structure influences the bank growth of commercial banks in Tanzania?
iii. To what extent bank ownership structure influences the financial soundness of commercial banks in Tanzania?

One should also be carefully in formulating the research objectives. Each research objective formulated from the variables of the conceptual framework should easily reflect the independent variable and the dependent variable

6.3 Objectives of Conceptual Framework

The conceptual framework is designed as a kind of road map to follow so as to be able to conduct focused research capable of addressing specific research objectives and answering specific research questions. Without a clear conceptual framework, the research may become disorganized or unfocused.

A clear conceptual framework is useful in defining a clear scope of the study. It specifies just how far the research will go and puts limits and boundaries on the study.

It will also show easily identified independent variables in the study and how they are linked to each other. A strong conceptual framework is one with clearly defined independent, moderating, intervening and dependent variables. Some studies may incorporate all variables together and in cases such as these, the conceptual framework must be articulated without confusion or the actual research will become difficult to undertake. These variables can help in formulating specific research objectives and specific research questions. Each independent variable, moderating variable, intervening variable should be linked to the subsequent dependent variable.

6.4 Operationalization of the Conceptual Framework Research Variables

Operationalizing the conceptual framework is all about breaking down what is contained in the conceptual framework from general to specific. There are many types of variables. However, operationalization of the research variable is important at it helps to define the exact study variable of the current study. It makes the study hypothesis strong and clear while also standardizing the variables used in the research.

In this case, a student will need to define the independent, moderating, intervening, and dependent variables of their study and support them with a quality literature review and empirical evidence. Once this has all been defined, other scholars and researchers should be mentioned who have also used the same variables in the previous studies. The explanation of the study variables includes definitions as per existing literature. It is also good to state how the study will adopt these variables, whether 100% adoption from previous studies or slight modification from previous studies.

The modification of variables from previous studies has to be justified with reasons supported fully within the literature review or other important reasons prevailing from the environment surrounding the current study. Consider the conceptual framework diagrammed above in Figure 6.1 with one independent variable (Bank Ownership) and four dependent variables (Service Quality, Bank Growth, Bank Efficiency and Bank Profitability). In this case one would have to discuss all of the variables within the conceptual framework.

6.4.1 Key variables in the Conceptual Framework

A key question many researchers will ask themselves is, *"Should my study include all the variables?"*. The answer to this question is simple. Not every research topic will include all variables. It depends completely on the type of the study one chooses and the depth of that study. Daniel (2012) indicates that the most commonly used variables in research are the independent and dependent variables. If a student has a short time to complete his or her thesis, less variables should be studied. Resource availability, data availability and whether the study is at the master's or doctorate level will influence a student's decision about which variables to include.

6.4.2 Independent Variable

Evert (2002) defines the independent variable as the key variable that is changed or controlled in a research experiment and states that it represents the cause or reason for an outcome. In other words, we can similarly define the independent variable as a driver, input or an assumption that can be changed or controlled in order to assess its influence or impact on a dependent variable (Corporate Finance Institute 2020). The term independent variable can also be seen as an input and the dependent variable as an outcome. According to Crossman and Ashley (2020), the independent variable is usually hypothesized to be the cause of the dependent variable and research is conducted to prove whether the hypothesis is true or not. Mwasele and Bradina (2000) define an independent variable as a variable which, when known, can be used to predict the value of a dependent variable.

In this section of the thesis, as a student one is expected to define the independent variable and show how it links to the study's dependent variable. If there is more than one independent variable, they should be explained one by one.

Empirical discussion is important in this section to show the linking of research variables. The empirical discussion should focus on the particular independent variables selected and their relative dependent variables.

It is also important to review the literature to show any empirical evidence of the relationship between the independent and dependent variables hypothesized in the current study. Also, which measurements were used to measure the independent variable in the previous studies and in the current study are important to mention.

It is likely that the current research topic is not new or totally unique and, therefore, it is important to show how previous studies established the relationship between the variables in the current study. Finally, the discussion in this section should end by stating the expected relationship between the selected independent and dependent variables in the study.

6.4.3 Dependent Variable

The dependent variable is defined as the variable that responds to changes in the independent variable (Evert 2002). Mwasele and Baradyana (2000) define the dependent variable as a variable which depends on the other variable(s) called independent variable(s). This, in essence means, the dependent variable is completely dependent on the independent variable. It is the variable which should be measured and how it is affected by the independent variable will be observed. Therefore, in this section a clear definition of the dependent variable and how it is impacted by the independent variable is necessary. In some studies, there may be more than one dependent variable and so it must be clearly laid out how these variables will be measured.

6.4.4 Intervening Variable

Some studies, depending on their nature, may have intervening variables in addition to the dependent and independent variables. For intervening variables, the researcher may be interested to see how these variables influence both the independent and dependent variables. In cases such as these, it is important to be clear in establishing the research objectives to show a proper link between the variables using a flow-chart or other diagram.

6.4.5 Moderating Variable

This variable is considered to have moderating effects on the strength of relationship between an independent variable and dependent variable. Lai (2013) defines a moderating variable as the variable that affects the strength or direct ion of connotation between another independent variable and an outcome variable. Moderating effects are characterized by the ability of the third variable to change the relationship between two related variables.

In business research for example market turbulences, company size, industry type, organizational culture, organization structure and many other factors are considered to have moderating effects on organizational performances (Rayees and Sandip, 2017). In the same way as independent variable and dependent variables, moderating variables should be clearly defined and explained with proper empirical literature support when operationalizing the variables of the conceptual framework. It is also critical to explain or show how the study will measure the moderating variable. It is also important to show how the moderating variable is linked to the dependent variable; therefore, it is also important to formulate a research objective and research questions that links the two variables (moderating variable and dependent variable) and design research instruments that can help to gather necessary information that can help to answer the research question related to these two variables.

6.5 Defining the Measurement of the Research Variable

Each research variable selected for a study needs explanation. The explanation will include the proper definition of the variable as supported by proper literature, measurement of the variable from previous empirical literature as well as the researchers own choice of measurement for the current study. This means that the current student should show how previous studies used the variable compared to how it will be used in the current study. A table that summarizes the measurement types and supporting literature will be useful in this instance.

Consider the following example of the study topic *"**The Influence of Liquidity on Capital structure of Tanzanian Companies (Yona 2018)**.* In this case, the independent variable of the study is liquidity and the dependent variable is capital structure. The following explanation of the variables were given to define liquidity and define its measurement.

Liquidity

According to Ghasema and Ab Razak (2016), liquidity is the key indicator that measures whether the company can fulfil its debts commitment by using its liquid assets. There are different measures of the liquidity namely current ratio (CR) and the Quick ratio (QR). In this study, Liquidity is measured by using current ratio. This is the measure of the extent to which the company can meet its current maturing obligation by using its liquid resources. (Yona, 2018)

$$\text{CURRENT RATIO} = \frac{\text{CURRENT ASSETS}}{\text{CURRENT LIABILITIES}}$$

Table 3.1 Proxy Measurement of Independent Variables

Variable	Measurement	Comparable Study
Size	logarithm of net sales	Padron et al (2005)
Liquidity	Current RATIO = Current Assets / Current Liabilities	Submitter and Anderson (2002) Ankilo (2011), Ahmed and Arris (2015)

Source: Yona (2018): Factors influencing Leverage of Tanzanian Companies

Measuring the dependent variable (Leverage)

In this study, leverage was the dependent variable. The study used book value debt to equity ratio and debt ratio as measures of leverage (Capital structure) for both unlisted and listed companies in Tanzania. We defined leverage as debt to equity ratio which is total liabilities divided by equity plus total debt and debt ratio as total debt divided by total equity. This measurement is consistent with other studies on capital structure.

Table 3.2. Proxy Measurement for Dependent Variable (Capital Structure)

Variable	Measurement	Comparable Study
Debt to Equity Ratio	$\dfrac{\text{Total Debts}}{\text{Total Equity + Total Debts}}$	Hall et al. (2006)
Debt Ratio	$\dfrac{\text{Total Debts}}{\text{Total Equity}}$	Correia et al. (2006)

Source: Researcher 2017

6.6 Challenges in formulating the conceptual framework

Formulating the conceptual framework is a key factor in any research thesis. However, this section of thesis development can be difficult for students and several challenges should be expected and accounted for. Overcoming these challenges will make the conceptual framework much stronger.

The following are some of the most common challenges which students experience when trying to formulate the conceptual framework for a research thesis:

- No clear understanding of what the conceptual framework is or what it is expected to achieve.
- An inability to link the conceptual framework with the research questions, research objective and the research topic.

- Clouded conceptual framework diagram which makes it difficult to determine the independent and dependent variables.
- Inability to define and explain the independent and dependent variable
- Inability to come up with clear operationalization of these variables
- Difficulties in explaining how the independent and dependent variables were measured in previous studies and how they will be measured in the current study
- A complete lack of a conceptual framework
- Inadequately labelled research variables in the conceptual framework

6.7 Organization of the Conceptual Framework Chapter

As mentioned above, the conceptual framework can be discussed separately as a separate chapter of its own or combined with the research methodology chapter. The choice depends mostly on the directives of the examining university. However, for master's degree studies, if dictated to be a certain format, the best option is to combine it with the research methodology. However, for doctoral theses, it is advantageous to dedicate a chapter to the conceptual framework alone so that all elements can be discussed in detail. The recommended practice is to dedicate some sections for each of the key variables in the conceptual framework as outlined below.

3.1 Introduction
3.2 Conceptual Framework
3.3 Operationalization of the research Variable
    3.3.1 Independent variable
    3.3.2 Dependent Variable
    3.3.3 Moderating Variable or Intervening Variable
    3.3.4 Proxy Measurement of the Research Variables
3.4 Chapter Conclusion

The above order can still change if the conceptual framework discussions are combined with the research methodology. You need to adhere to the requirements of the examining university. However, there is no much change on the contents of the conceptual framework mentioned here but only that the conceptual framework discussion will precede before explanations of the research methodology.

6.8　Conclusion

The chapter has explained the role the conceptual framework in any research work. It addresses how formulate the conceptual framework and operationalize the study variables. The chapter emphasizes the importance of defining the research variables with support of empirical literature and showing how the study should measure those variables. Furthermore, the chapter has highlighted a few challenges which students experience in formulating their conceptual frameworks.

Practice Question

Question 1

Discuss why the conceptual framework is an important element of any research

Question 2

What is included in the operationalization of the conceptual framework and why is it important?

Question 3

What is expected in the discussion of the independent and dependent variables?

Question 4

What are the main characteristics of a great research hypothesis?

Question 5

Discuss the challenges in formulating an appropriate research hypothesis.

Question 6

Why should one look back at their literature review while formulating their research hypothesis?

CHAPTER 7
DESIGNING THE RESEARCH METHODOLOGY

7.1 Introduction

The research methodology chapter is a key chapter because it explains the methods one uses to collect and analyze the research data. It should be noted that some business schools and universities prefer to combine the conceptual framework and research methodology into one chapter (Conceptual Framework and Research Methodology) while others prefer, they are separated. Since there are no agreed upon international standards about this, students should follow the guidelines given by the institution they will be presenting their research to. This book will discuss the conceptual framework and research methodology separately and so this chapter will deal only with the methodology section.

To start off, let's discuss the importance of clear language usage both during the proposal and through to the completion of the thesis. Students should ensure accuracy in their use of tenses throughout the document at all stages. At the research proposal stage, it is appropriate to use the future tense and when the research is complete, the past tense is required. Students often make the mistake of using the future tense even when the research is complete or mistakenly us past tense at the proposal stage. Both of these tense usage problems should be checked for and corrected before thesis submission at each stage.

In addition to language usage, the methods one adopts to collect and analyze their research data should be pertinent to the research objectives and research questions. This chapter aims to explain and discuss the research design, study population, study area, sampling method, sample size, data collection methods, data analysis, data reliability and validity, hypothesis formulation, hypothesis testing, and ethical considerations.

7.2 Research Design

In this section the student is expected to explain the research design that will guide the study. According to Gilbert et al. (2002), a research design is a plan for a study or, in other words, a framework that can help an individual to collect and analyze his or her data. It resembles an architectural blueprint in that it makes the research easier to conduct. A strong research design also improves efficiency as a plan is in place which researchers use to follow in collecting and analyzing the data. However, we should note that there are different types of research design which an individual can choose for his or her research. Table 7.1 below summarizes different types of research designs one can adopt or combine to best fit the research data collection needs and meet the research objectives.

Table 7.1 Types of Research Design

Type of Research	Definition and Key Issues
Explanatory Research	- More emphasize on gaining discovery of ideas and insights - Breaking broad and vague statements into smaller or precise subproblems statements - increase familiarity with the problem, clarify concepts, clarify notions - developing hypothesis - Explanatory research is appropriate to any problem about which little is known (Gilbert et al 2002) - Less Use of detailed questionnaires rather flexible with more use of literature survey, focus groups and analysis of case studies

Descriptive Research	These types of study are used in the following circumstances - when one wants to describe the characteristics of certain groups - when estimating the proportion of people in a specified population who behave in a certain way - when making specific prediction - Types (Longitudinal Studies or Cross-Sectional Studies)
Casual Research	- aims at determining the cause effect relationships, takes forms of field experiments and laboratory experiments - concentrates in providing evidence regarding the cause relationships between variables by means of time order in which variables occur and concomitant variations (Gilbert et al 2002)

Source: Gilbert et al 2002

The following example below illustrates how the research design can be documented into a thesis. The sample has been picked from the study we have continued to look back at "***The Impact of Bank Ownership on Banking Competitiveness: Case of Tanzanian Banks***" (Yona 2016). The study was an explanatory case study of commercial banks in Tanzania which required both quantitative and qualitative data.

Box 7.1 Example of Research Design

> "This was a case study, which used both quantitative and qualitative data from primary and secondary sources. This study adopts a cross-sectional survey of the bank customers in four regions in Tanzania namely Arusha, Kilimanjaro, Mwanza and Dar-Es-Salaam and it takes into consideration of the big size of the country which has more than twenty-five regions. These regions represent the major cities in the country having a majority of the banking population. The study administered structured questionnaires to walk in customers of both private and semi-quasi banks to collect the required information; however, it excluded all corporate bank customers. The questionnaires were also administered to selected bank officials of private and semi-quasi banks. The study also used quantitative data, obtained from the financial statements of the banks for the six years between year 2006 and year 2011 plus other bank information obtained from the Bank of Tanzania."

Yona (2016): The *I*mpact of Bank ownership on Banking Competitiveness

7.3 Study Population

When one hears the term study population, it should be clear that what is being referred to is the target population one intends to study (Umar 2018). Though it is not possible to include an entire population in a research study, one should establish a representative sample of the total population and thereafter generalize the research findings of the total sample to the entire population. In defining the study population, it is important to describe the demographic characteristics such as the age, marital status, sex, level of education, work status and any other information which is relevant.

Since it is not possible to include an entire population in a study, there is a need from the beginning of the research design to define the inclusion and exclusion criteria in order to ensure that there is no data interference from non-participants in the research. The inclusion criteria should define the characteristics that allows a participant as an individual or entity to join the research student and exclusion criteria explains when individuals or entities are not appropriate for the study.

Box 7.2 Sample of Study Population Descriptions

> **Study Population**
> The population of this study comprised of all commercial banks in Tanzania which were already registered by the Bank of Tanzania (BOT) by the end of year 2010. Since the number of banks was below 50, the study will consider all 32 banks which were registered by the Bank of Tanzania by the end of year 2010 as the total population the study. Tanzania had a total number of 32 commercial banks by end of year 2010. At the same time, the population will include all bank customers of all the commercial banks under the study.

Source: Yona (2016)

7.4   Study area

When looking at a study area, a researcher is looking at exactly what physical area will be studied. The methodology chapter should explain where the study participants will be concentrated and should provide a detailed description of the area and rationalization for the selection of the study area. It should be clear why and how you chose your study area and what alternatives you did not choose with justification for their exclusion.

The description of the study area might include information such as the physical area measurements (in square kilometers), the population, literacy rate and administrative set-up. Obviously, the factors that should be described will differ depending on the scope and specifics of the study one conducting. In the study of Yona (2016), the study area was limited to three regions in Tanzania and the reasons as to why these regions were selected are outlined in Box 7.2 below. The example is not exhaustive of what needs to be included in this section because, as already mentioned, the requirements will differ depending on the research specifics but hopefully the example will provide a model from which students can begin creating their study area descriptions.

Box 7.3 Example of Study Area Explanation

> The study area for this research study included Dar-es-salaam, Arusha, Moshi and Mwanza, Tanzania. The choice of Dar-es-salaam was because the majority of the commercial banks in Tanzania are headquartered here. Arusha, Moshi and Mwanza were selected because they are prominent cities in the with more economic activities than other cities in Tanzania and so are likely to have more bank customers than other regions. The research collected primary data from customers and bank officials of thirty-two Tanzanian commercial banks which were already registered by the Bank of Tanzania (BOT) by the end of year 2010. To date, Tanzania has a total number of fifty-three banks, thirty-two banks were registered before 2010 and remaining banks thereafter.

Source: Yona (2016)

7.5 Sampling Method

Since it is not possible to use the whole population in a study, especially when the population is particularly large, picking a sample that accurately represents the total population becomes important. The critical issue to consider is exactly how to know if a sample is truly representative or not. Samples which are too large may be costly and time-consuming to research but samples which are too small will not yield representative or useful results. Therefore, it is important to pick a good sample by using an appropriate sampling method. There are several different sampling methods which one can use to select a quality sample.

In this section of the thesis, students need to describe the type of sampling methods which were selected and utilized. In addition to mentioning these samples, there must be a clear justification for these methods and an explanation of how the sampling method has created a representative sample. To be able to make this explanation, a student researcher must have an adequate understanding of a variety of sampling methods and the conditions which each method can and should be used prior to choosing a sampling method for his or her research thesis.

Some examples of commonly used sampling methods are simple random sampling, systematic sampling, random route sampling, stratified random sampling, quota sampling, cluster sampling and multi-stage sampling (Tim 1997). Each of these methods are applicable under certain conditions. In this chapter section, the student is not expected to explain the theoretical background which supports each sampling method but rather should focus on methods considered and ultimately selected for the current study. Students tend discuss a large number of sampling methods which is not necessary as they are not relevant to the study at hand.

Box 7.4 Sample of Sampling Descriptions

> Stratified random sampling was used to pick the representative sample of bank customers and bank officials who will provide answers on perception on bank economic and quality efficiency in Tanzania. Stratified sampling was used because banks customers and bank officials are located in different regions where the banks operate.

Source: Yona 2016

7.6 Sample Size

Donald (2001) defines a sample as a group of cases, respondents or records comprised of part of the target population, carefully selected to represent that population. In this section of the report, as a researcher, one needs to state clearly what the total sample size is and explain how it was picked from the total population. The sample size is always independent from the total population. The literature reveals that a sample size depends on the resources and time available as well as the degree of accuracy required and variability of the population (Tim 1997). In determining one's sample size one should also consider their research objectives, define the sample population, unit, sample frame, and decide on a survey method. Lastly the researcher will choose the sampling method.

Box 7.5 Sample size and Sampling Frame

Sample size

In selecting the sample size for this study, purposefully sampling will be more appropriate. There are 32 Banks in Tanzania which were registered by Bank of Tanzania prior to year 2010, (Table 2.1), therefore clustering the banks into two major group's namely semi quasi banks and private banks was taken into consideration. In order to obtain the answers on the research questions and achieve the desired research objectives, a bank survey was designed specific for bank officials and bank customers. A total number of 224 bank officials in their different positions (Table 4.1) were expected to respond to the structured questionnaires designed to provide answers to all research questions

Table 4.1 Sampling Frame for Bank official Survey

Respondents	Number of expected respondents in each bank
Chief Executive Officer (1 in each bank)	32
Chief Financial Officers (1 in each bank)	32
Middle Level Managers (4 in each bank)	128
Finance Officers/Accountants (1 in each bank)	32
Total	**224**

Source: Research Data Base 2014

In order to obtain answers on perception of customers on banking competitiveness of commercial bank in Tanzania, a total number of 1600 of customers, 50 from each of the 32 banks were expected to respond to the structured questionnaires (Table 4.2)

Table 4.2 Sampling Frame for Bank Customers Survey

Respondents expected from each bank	Sample of expected response from customers
50 Customers from each bank	1600
Total	**1600**

Source: Research Data Base 2014

Source: Yona 2016

7.7 Data Collection Methods

There are different ways of collecting data depending on the data needed whether qualitative or quantitative. In research data collection, one needs to use several different measurement tools to achieve the research objectives and answer the research questions.

Research instruments are aids or tools that can help the researcher to gather information that will help him to answer the research questions and achieve the research questions. The instruments can help in the process of gathering the respective information and gather data that are important to address the research questions of the study.

Types of Data

There are different types of research data that you may be required to gather, which are categorized as primary or secondary data. Each of the data types is important for you to complete your thesis.

Primary Data

Primary data is gathered by the researcher from the original source. Kabir and Syed (2016) emphasize that primary data should be collected from firsthand experiences, not collected from published sources. It should be authentic and reliable and not changed at any stage of collection. Sources of primary data may include experiments, questionnaires, surveys, interviews and observations

Secondary Data

Secondary data is considered to be secondhand data-- already collected by other people in the past, processed and published. Secondary data may include secondary statistics or past financial reports, budgetary reports etc. therefore, it is essential that you have to dig more about them to know how they were collected, processed and whether they are accurate and reliable to use them. The use of secondary data in your research can be cheap and easily available but you have to be carefully how do you use such data (Hannagan, 1997). Sources of secondary data include books, newspapers and published research papers.

7.8 Types of Research Instruments

There are various research instruments that are useful for information collection. Depending on the type of the study, one can utilize two or more tools to improve the validity and reliability of the information collected. David W and Peter (2003) dedicated an entire book to discussing various types of research instruments which one can use to gather the necessary information. The methods discussed include

- A. Questionnaires
- B. Interviews
- C. Content Analyses
- D. Focus Groups
- E. Observations
- F. Researching the things people say and do
- G. Tests

It is important in this section to discuss briefly these types of research instrument in order to help you to understands the methods, the circumstances to use the method, the benefits and diastase of each method.

7.8.1 Questionnaires

Questionnaires are designed to help gather primary data in research work. The design of questionnaires is critical: it is possible to ask questions which are out of context, difficult for responders to understand, or questions which are confusing and fail to provide answers which can be used in understanding the if the research objectives were met or not. Researchers should remember when asking a question requiring a response, each question should be useful in answering the predetermined research questions and in achieving one's research objectives. Questions should not be ambiguous or wordy but should be simple and clear for any responder to answer effectively. Questionnaires can be structured in different ways through the inclusion of open-ended (unstructured) or closed-ended (structured) questions or even a combination of the two (Richard and Schmidt 2002). Questionnaires are great tools for researchers because, with up-to-date statistical analysis software, data can be analyzed quickly.

Open-ended questionnaires

Open ended questionnaires include questions that are not structured to elicit specific answers. They don't give pre-determined answers and are not suggestive. Using open-ended questions allows responders to understand the questions and provide answers as they see fit. They create space for respondents to give their opinions. While these questionnaires can be difficult to collate, they provide information that is deeper and wider than what can be obtained through other methods.

Examples of open-ended questions

1. Tell us some of the reasons as to why people in your area prefer to buy Dell computers rather than Toshiba computers.
2. What do you think the best option for Kenya would have been for the COVID-19 crisis?

Closed-ended questionnaires

These questionnaires include structured questions with expected answers from respondents. In other words, the respondent has no room to give any answers beyond the prepared responses designed by the researcher. The designer of the questions may suggest possible answers with a few alternatives and the responder has no option to provide an answer beyond the suggested answers.

Examples of closed-ended questions

1. Dichotomous questions that require Yes or No answers such as:
    Have you been rejected entrance into Tanzania in the last 10 years?

2. Multiple choice questions which provide several answer options from which the responder chooses one such as in which of these cities do you find doing business the most difficult?
   A. Mwanza;
   B. Arusha;
   C. Dar es Salaam;
   D. Tanga

Ranking order Scaling

These questionnaires use a less common questioning technique-ranking order scaling questions. These questions require responders to rank the alternative solution based on certain attributes or characteristics. For example, Rank the following computer brands from best quality to poorest quality: Dell, Mac, Toshiba, and Dell. In ranking scaling questions, respondents must not be allowed to announce a tie between items. They must be ranked with values attached to each ranking placement.

Mixed Questionnaires: In these types of questionnaires, the respondent is given both open and closed-end questions. This is a great alternative when a variety of information is required.

7.8.2 Interviews

Interviews are structured conversations between an interviewer and respondents about a specific topic. The answers for the designed questions are not pre-determined but questions can be pre-determined with some flexibility to add additional questions as the interview flows.

Interviews can be structured or unrestructured. Structured interviews are those where an interviewer uses structured questions with respondents to seek answers on a specific topic. The answers from the designed questions are not pre-determined, but the questions are. Respondents are not given options to choose their answers from but instead they respond based on their own understanding of the questions.

Interviews are useful in research contexts where other instruments such as questionnaires are inadequate or inappropriate for the data needs.

A research instrument may not be able to provide the right and appropriate answers for the specific research questions. Inappropriate could also mean that the inability of the respondents to give appropriate answers to structured questions due to a language barrier or skills.

To conduct a good interview, one must start with a strong draft of the interview questions. Asking appropriate questions in the interview should help researchers to achieve one's research objectives and answer the research questions. Asking the wrong questions and so receiving inadequate answers can make it difficult for researchers to get the information they need. The next stage of the process is to pilot the interview questions to test whether they elicit the needed responses. Thereafter, it is important to select the sample of interviews and conduct the interview. Once the interview is complete, then proper analysis of interview data follows, and eventually, final report can be developed.

7.8.3 Focus Group

A focus group involves a discussion between two parties which is guided by structured and unstructured questions on a specific topic. Anderson (1996) defines a focus group as a carefully planned and moderated informal discussion where one person's ideas bounce off another's creating a chain reaction of informative dialogue.

In a focus group discussion, there are structured open-ended questions which address a specific topic or research theme in depth. Its purpose is to address a specific topic in order to encourage members in the discussion to give a wide range of opinions on subject matters related to the study. Focus group discussions are normally expected to give qualitative information which creates wider and broader knowledge and understanding by respondents about the subject matter under discussion.

In order for a focus group discussion to be effective in meeting the research objectives and needs of the research questions, the right questions must be asked. Asking the wrong questions confuses the study and wastes the time of the researcher. The choice of appropriate individuals in the focus group is also of paramount importance. Choosing the wrong participants for the focus group will provide inadequate answers and may confuse the study.

It is very useful for focus group discussion to have a clearly established and adhered to start and finish time. A mixture of different of individuals from different demographics helps avoid bias and opens the space for more depth of discussion and answers.

7.8.4 Observation

Observation is all about watching or looking physically at what others are doing as related to specific issues that a researcher is interested in. While carrying out an observation, observed participants may or may not be aware that they are being observed. Merriam (1998) emphasizes for need for a researcher to focus on the research objective and research questions in order to have a focused observation. DeWalt and DeWalt (2002) argue that when conducting observations, one needs to focus on what is happening and why, sort out the regular from irregular activities, look for variations to view the event from a variety of viewpoints and look for negatives and exceptions observations.

Observations can be grouped into three groups namely controlled observation, participants observations and Naturalistic Observation. Therefore, it shows that the type of the study decides whether observation method can be applicable or not.

Controlled observation

Controlled observations require a random selection of participants to be observed. The researcher should explain the research aim to participants and determined place of observation and pre-determined time for observations be established and utilized.

Controlled observations are commonly used in scientific health related studies or laboratory research. There is a danger of obtaining unreliable observation data because participants have been found to change their behavior during the period of observation especially when they are informed of the research goals.

Participant observation

In this type of observation, the observer is also a participant in the process. DeWalt (2002) defines participant observation as a process that enables researchers to learn the activities of the people under study in natural settings through observing and participating in the observed activities themselves.

DeWalt and DeWalt (2002) further argue that the importance of this method is that it helps researchers develop a holistic understanding of the issues being studied and adds validity of the study.

Participatory observation has many benefits such as:

- It allows richly detailed descriptions and provides opportunities for participating in unscheduled events (DeMunk and Sobo,1998)
- It improves quality of data collection and interpretation and facilitates the development of new research questions and hypothesis (DeWalt and DeWalt, 2002)
- It enables the researcher to collect both quantitative and qualitative data through surveys and interviews (Bernard,1994)

Naturalistic Observation

Naturalistic observation is more applicable in data collection in social and behaviour studies. Cozy (2009) defines it as the process of observing and recording data in natural setting. The observation is targeted towards behaviour of specific variables, issues under the study in order to provide answers to the research question. Naturalistic observation is a process of observing and recording the pattern of behaviour of certain characteristics or variables under study. In naturalistic approach, people, cultural settings, other subjects are observed in natural settings. It also supports the study of cultural settings and subjects that couldn't be studied in other ways. However, naturalistic observation is unable to control the variables and its results lacks replicability.

7.9 Factors to Consider when Choosing Research Instruments

The decisions to use a specific research instrument to gather information depends on number of factors including:

a. ***The nature of the study:*** Studies which require qualitative or quantitative data will use different research instruments.
b. ***Validity and reliability of data:*** Mohamed (2013) argues the importance of using mixed data collection methods to boost the validity and reliability of data.
c. ***Type of respondents:*** Who are you gathering information from and why?
d. ***Time frame for the study.*** Longer period study will influence the method on how you will collect your data.

7.10 Qualities of Good Research Instruments

Each research instrument chosen for data collection has its own advantages and disadvantages. However, there are some specific qualities an instrument should possess to be considered a good research instrument as highlighted below.

a. **Appropriateness:** Can it meet the research need; help provide answers to research questions and achieve the objectives of the research?
b. **Comprehensibility for respondents:** Can respondents understand the questions asked without any support or explanation?
c. **Keep language simple and avoid technical jargon:** Is your language choice appropriate for the respondents or does it include too much technical jargon for the general public to understand?
d. **Avoid long and complicated questions**

e. **Avoid asking questions which do not assist in answering the main and specific research questions**
f. **Consider mixed questioning techniques:** Can you really get all of the information needed with just one type of questioning? If not, combine several research techniques

7.11 Challenges in designing research instruments

Designing research instruments that are likely to help the researcher to achieve the research objectives is of paramount importance though with challenges, one might design weak instruments that might be irrelevant. The following noted challenges requires special attention:

A. Asking too many questions that are repetitive in nature
B. Asking Too many questions with Yes and No answers.
C. Having too many questions which are not relevant or appropriate to the study itself
D. Having questions which do not address the key variables of the study
E. Using data collection methods which are not relevant to the study
F. Using inappropriate language that cannot be easily understood by the respondents
G. Using technical jargon which are not simplified to meet the abilities of users
H. Use of biased questions that doesn't allow respondents to give their true opinions

7.12 Data Analysis

This section is meant to explain how the researcher will analyze his or her data, whether qualitative or quantitative with the support of statistical techniques. The use of tables, graphs and charts to explain research data which has been analyzed is of paramount importance in this section. The analysis should explain and inform readers about the mean, modes, standard deviation, certain for and explain analyzed your qualitative data.

Data collection without analysis is essentially useless as unanalyzed data cannot serve to answer research questions no meet the research objectives. Therefore, it is important to analyze all data collected through different research instruments. Shamoo and Resnick (2003) explain data analysis as the process of using statistical and logical techniques to explain, condense and evaluate data. The data can be primary or secondary data. Data analysis is a process of combination of number of activities that a researcher needs to do in order to explore data and find meaning out of them. It also requires one need to use data analysis tools and software's which can help to interpret and present data in understandable way to readers.

Data analysis, therefore, involves simplifying data collected from different sources so that readers can understand trends and interpret and draw conclusions from the data for informed decision-making.

The process of data analysis should be continuous as data is collected until the completion of the study (Savenye and Robinson, 2004). This makes the analysis work easy for researchers as they do not have to analyze large amounts of data at the end of their study but rather little by little as the study develops and is conducted.

The objective of data analysis is to generate useful and usable information. The expectation of data analysis process is to describe and summarize data, identify relationships between variables, compare those variables and identify differences between them so that inferences can be made.

7.13 Techniques to Analyze data

There are various techniques that can be used to analyze data collected through research instruments. Data analysis techniques depend on whether a study is qualitative or quantitative in nature and each technique is unique. Specific instruments are suited for specific types of data analysis and information gain. We discuss below the data analysis for both qualitative studies as well as for quantitative studies.

7.13.1 *Qualitative studies*

Qualitative studies are more explanatory studies which seek to provide answers to how and why questions related to study variables. These studies do not involve numerical data, but rather the collection of data from focus group discussions, interviews, documents, surveys, pictures and other sources. Qualitative studies collect vast of information from different sources, reduce, summarize and interpret the information so as to give proper meaning to the data in a structured manner.

In order to analyze the vast amount of data a qualitative study creates, reducing data must be prioritized. Pope et al. (2000) defines data reduction as the process of examining vast amounts of data with a pre- determined framework that reflects your aims, research interest and objectives in mind. It requires researchers to focus on particular answers and abandon others during the data analysis—a process called framework analysis.

Attride-strings (2001) suggests another method for reducing qualitative data which involves coding all data and allowing new impressions to shape the interpretation of data in different and unexpected directions. Coding of qualitative data requires the researcher to be quite familiar with the data and to make clear notes while analyzing the data. After this stage a summary of each transcript or piece of data is written. The researcher will use the summaries to sort the obtained I information into themes and topics for extraction.

7.13.2 *Quantitative studies*

Quantitative studies generate numerical data which can be in form of scores and ranking, units, ratios, proportion and percentages or prices. Collection of quantitative data is conducted using methods previously discussed including surveys and questionnaires, project records, financial statements and other quantitative indicators. Quantitative analysis is considered to be the most accurate type of analysis, but the accuracy of quantitative data is not guaranteed as it is depending on the quality of the analysis (Shamoo and Resnik 2003).

One should differentiate between several types of quantitative data available to them including categorical or numerical data. Categorizing the data makes it easier to analyze correctly. Categorical data includes such data as sex (male/female), quality of training (good, bad, average) whereas numerical data is purely in the form of numbers such as counts (number of customers at training), measures (height, weight of a child) or duration (time spent, age etc.).

7.14 Tools for Data Analysis

There are different types of tools for analyzing data, some are simple to use, and some are more complex that requires a specialization knowledge. However, even if one doesn't have specialization knowledge, can still use them to analyze data with a support from experts, such as statisticians.

Data analysis is easily supported by statistical tools such as spreadsheets to create basic graphs and statistical analysis packages such as SPPS, STATA NVivo and others. Each of the tools can be appropriate based on the types of data the choice of any data analysis tool depends so much on:

a. Availability of data
b. The types of data one needs to analyze
c. Complexity of data: More complex data might require a specialized tool for analysis
d. Ability and knowledge of the researcher to use the data analysis software
e. Ability of the researcher to give proper interpretation of the results

7.15 Data Presentation

The presentation of data matters a lot in research work. Both qualitative and quantitative data, after analysis must be presented in such a way that the audience reading the final report can understand the information presented. The thesis presentation should be catered to a specific audience, the objectives set, data gathering, and the analysis undertaken. Students should take care to ensure that their presentations don't overstate the evidence.

Presentation can take different forms including the use of graphs, charts, tables and figures with the support of clear explanation. All graphs, pictures, charts and tables should be labeled properly and given adequate explanation for correct interpretation by readers.

7.15.1 Table Presentation

In Box 9.1, examples of table presentation are found and followed by explanations of the table for previous studies (Yona 2016). Tables can be created in terms of frequency distribution to explain how often each value of the research variable in question in data set appears.

Explanation of a table's contents and purpose should be provided directly before the inclusion of a table. A table with no explanation should never be found in a thesis and in table explanations, the table name or number must always be clarified. The table should be labeled at the top and should include the source of the table below. It may be beneficial to combine a number of tables in order to have fewer tables as done in the example below. It was possible to come up with four separate tables but to avoid having too many tables, all four tables were combined into one. To combine tables, though, the data or information in the tables must be highly interconnected.

Box 7.6 Example of Table Presentations and Explanation

The study targeted a sample of one thousand six hundred (1,600) customers of all commercial banks designed for the study, and the response was 838 (60%). According to the results (Table 4.1) responses came from customers of both private banks and semi-quasi banks. Of all customers' responses, 25% were customers from private banks and 75% from semi-quasi banks. In terms of the bank locations, customers were from Kilimanjaro (56%), Arusha (14%), Dar-Es-Salaam (19%) and Mwanza (10%). The majority of respondents were male (61%) and female were thirty seven percent (39%). The respondent's age group ranged from age of 18 years to sixty years (60) with the majority between 18 and 29 years (48%).

Table 5.1 - Demographic Characteristics-Bank Customers

Bank Ownership	Frequency	Percent
Private	212	25.1
Semi Quasi	627	74.7
Total	**838**	**99.9**
Location	Frequency	Percent
Mwanza	8	10.4
Arusha	161	19.2
Dar-es-salaam	123	14.7
Kilimanjaro	467	55.7
Total	**838**	**99.9**
Gender of Customers	Frequency	Percent
Male	514	60.9
Female	325	38.6
Total	**839**	**99.9**
Age of Customers	Frequency	Percent
< 18 years	15	1.8
Btw 19 years and 29	401	47.8
Btw 30 years and 40	249	29.7
Btw 41years and 50	104	12.4
Btw 51 Years and 60	53	6.3
> 60 years	27	1.8
Total	**839**	**100**

Source: Yona (2016) The impact of Bank ownership on Banking Competitiveness

7.15.2 Graph Presentation

Bar charts or bar graphs are pictorial representations of data displayed in the form of horizontal or vertical bars. Normally the lengths of the bars represent the measure of the data.

There are other types of graphs which may also effectively display data. Some other types of graphs are vertical bar graphs, horizontal bar charts or range bar charts, etc. Each student should determine which type of graph will best display their data, always keeping in mind that the data should be easily understood by readers of all academic backgrounds. When deciding to present data in graph form, the same rules discussed above about tables should be followed. Give the explanations of the graph first and then show the graph with proper labelling and clear citation of the source of the graph. Below are several samples of data presentation in graph form from previous studies. Figure 8.1 below is a typical example of data presentation of customer age for a particular study. The age is grouped in range of years (X-Axis) and percentages of each group of years (Y-axis). However, the bar graphs are derived from data that are first tabulated in a table

Figure 7.1 Bar Graphs (Customer Age)

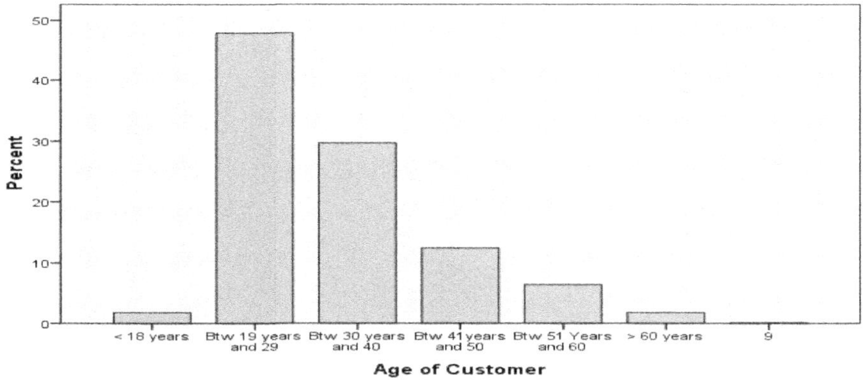

Source: Researcher (2016)

Line Graphs

Another graph presentation is the use of line graphs that can be derived from the summarized data. Line graphs are useful in showing the trend of series of data over time and can be helpful in comparing different situations, events and information. For example, under figure 8.2 two variables important variables are identified (Day and Degree of Fahrenheit in Mwanza City) to explain the temperature degree in Mwanza City (Tanzania) over selected weekdays. The variables are tabulated in a table (Table 7.1), thereafter these two variables are plotted in a graph, one being the independent variable (Day) plotted on x -axis and another being the degree of temperature in Fahrenheit plotted on the y-axis. After plotting the variables in point s, the points are joined by a line. (Figure 8.2)

Table 7. Temperature in Mwanza City (Fahrenheit)

Day	Degree in Fahrenheit
1	43
2	50
3	53
4	59
5	62
6	58
7	53

Source: Author

Figure 7.2 Temperature in Mwanza City

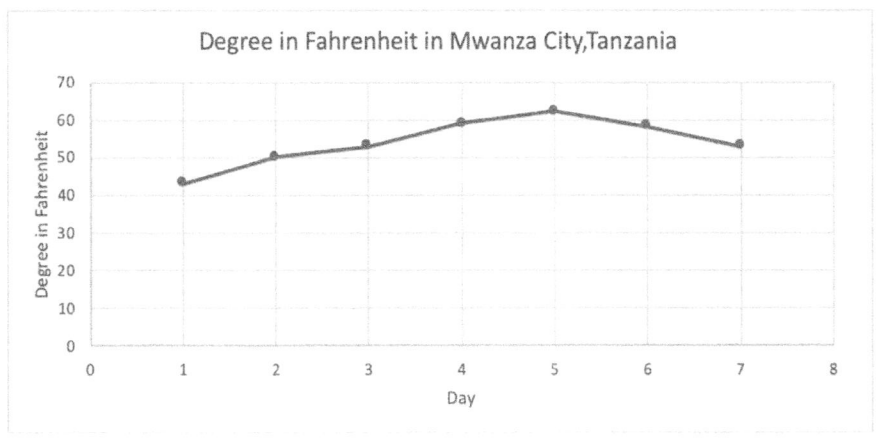

Source: Author 2020

Line graphs can be in multiple formats or scatter diagram too. The use of these types of line graphs depends so much on the kind of informations that one wants to present to his or her readers.

7.15.3 Pie Chart Presentations

Pie charts may also be used in presenting research data. They are considered to be good for presentation of data that show percentages or proportional. In pie chart presentation, the pie chart represents the whole of the data but pie is broken in slices. The pie charts slices will show different slices, but each one of the slices shows the percentage or proportional of the whole data. Pie charts are common in presenting in business and mass media arena. Pie charts present data in a simple way, they are easy to understand, interpret and hence make conclusions out of them.

The information provided under Box 8.1 above shows demographic data gathered from the study. Information on customer gender is tabulated in the table above which shows the number and percentage of female and male who participated in the study. Same information can be represented in a pie chart as depicted below under figure 8.3

Figure 7.3 Customer Gender

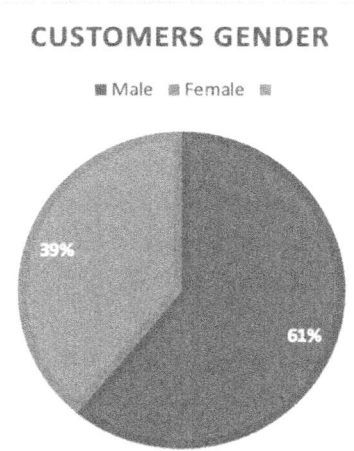

Source: Researcher 2016

7.16 Challenges in Data Analysis

Data analysis is clearly not an easy job especially for students who have little experience completing it. A number of challenges exist which may make data analysis to be difficult or may result in poor data analysis and hence poor data results. In order to ensure quality research results, these challenges have to be continually addressed until all research has been conducted and the thesis is ready for submission. The following are some of data analysis challenges to prepare for:

a. Lack of appropriate skills in data analysis such as use of statistical software's for data analysis;
b. Lack of clear objective outcomes from the analysis;
c. An inability to present data in a clear and proper manner;
d. An inability to provide honest and accurate data analysis;
e. An inability to use data analysis tools correctly; and
f. Having inappropriate subgroup analysis.

7.17 Data Reliability

Data reliability refers to the consistency of a measure to test the same thing each time (Petty R et al. 2009). Reliability may include dependability, consistency and precision. Reliability will also show the strength of the relationship between the test and its objective, reflecting that the test reflects what was reported to be tested (Glass, G.V 1996). In other words, reliability assures persons who access the research have confidence in the instrument used to gather data and to know that they can rely on the data collected. Of course, reliability takes different forms and statistical techniques to measure. Reliability can be defined in terms of results as compared to tests used or in terms of homogeneity of variables used in the study (internal consistency).

There are different techniques to test reliability such as the Cronbach Alpha and Cohen Kappa. These methods will be discussed below but to gain familiarity with other methods will require additional statistical book studies.

Cronbach's Alpha

Cronbach's Alpha is a test of internal consistency. This measures the reliability of the instrument in data collection. Reliability is normally measured by using Cronbach's Alpha test. The rule of thumb to use with this statistical measure is that the value of Cronbach's alpha should be >0.5 to give confidence of relying on the data. If Cronbach's Alpha is < 0.5 then it is concluded that there may be variable indicators which are not reliable for measuring the expected outcome and therefore a need to conduct a factor reduction analysis.

In a study by Yona and Inanga (2014), *Financial sector reforms in Bank Ownership and its Impact on Service Quality: Case of Commercial Banks in Tanzania*, Cronbach's Alpha was used to determine the reliability of service quality dimensions. Cronbach's Alpha was calculated in all measurements used to measure service quality. Reliability results are presented in Table 1. The coefficient results ranged from 0.512 to 0.873. This shows that the variables were reliable for testing the data and so there was no need of carrying further statistical tests or for removing any questionnaires from the study.

Box 7.7 Example: Data Reliability

Data reliability

Cronbach's Alpha was used to determine the reliability of service quality dimensions. Reliability is normally measured by using Cronbach's Alpha test. The rule of thumb is that the value of Cronbach's Alpha should be >0.5 to give confidence of relying on the data. If Cronbach alpha is < 0.5 then it is concluded that there may be variable indicators which are not reliable for measuring service quality and therefore a need to conduct a factor reduction analysis. Reliability results are presented in Table 1 below. The coefficient results range from 0.512 to 0. 873.This shows that our variables are reliable for testing our data and therefore no need of carrying further statistical test and removing any questionnaires from the study.

Table 1: Service Quality Reliability

Service Quality Dimension	Items	**Reliability Score (α)**
Tangibility	4	0.873
Reliability	4	0.793
Responsiveness	4	0.696
Assurance	4	0.512
Empathy	4	0.768

Source: Researcher 2016

In the above example, one can try to understand exactly what items and reliability scores are. The study used four questions about each area of service quality. The results show that all the questions in all four areas were reliable to determine service quality in all areas mentioned (tangibility, reliability, responsiveness, assurance and empathy).

Cohen Cappa

This is a measure of interrater reliability which measures the extent to which the data collected in the study are correct representation of the variable measured. The results of kappa statistics do range from -1 to +1 which shows the extent to which raters agree on the measurement. In other words, it is a measure which correlates each item with the other item and total scores. The results of Cappa helps to reveal weaker or stronger correlation between items. Those with weaker correlation can be removed showing low degree of homogeneity in the research instruments and leave those with strong correlation showing high degree of homogeneity. The higher the correlation the higher the degree of homogeneity. The interpretation of results means that values < 0 or equal to 0 indicates no agreement, and 0.01-0.20 as none to slight, 0.21 -0.40 as fair, 0.41-0.60 as moderate, 0.61-0.80 as substantial and 0.81-1.00 as almost perfect agreement between raters.

7.18 Data Validity

Data validity measures the extent to which the results of a study and the instruments used to obtain the data can be trusted. Data validity is more concerned with the integrity and quality of the research instrument (Kimberlin and Winter 2008). It shows the degree to which the research instrument is expected to correctly measure the concept under study. In other words, some instruments are not reliable for measuring specific concepts in the research study and so careful consideration when determining instruments to use is vital.

It is also important to distinguish validity in qualitative studies and validity in quantitative studies. In qualitative study, validity is all about checking the accuracy of the research findings (ChesWell, 2014) and in quantitative studies, validity is primarily concerned with checking the extent to which a research instrument measures what was intended to measure (Thatcher, 2010).

Another important thing in checking for data validity is to check for internal validity or external validity. There is internal validity where the study is legitimate and can be replicated (Wills, 2007) and whether the research findings can be attributed to the independent variable. Furthermore, internal validity is achieved if the researcher has applied different strategies in data collection such as triangulation, peer review or focus group discussion, or has used questionnaires. External validity is the extent to which the results achieved can be transferred to other groups of interest. Other aspects of external validity are on measuring the extent to which casual relationships can be generalized to different measures, settings and times (Allan and Kenneth 2008)

7.19 Hypothesis Formulation

Any student wishing to formulate a research hypothesis has to understand what the research hypothesis is, why the research hypothesis is important, and the attributes are of a good research hypothesis. A hypothesis is a statement that predicts the relationship between the research variables which requires a proof. Crossman and Ashley (2020) define a hypothesis as a specific statement of prediction that describes the concrete terms that are expected to occur in a study. However, such statements are not vague statements but are based solidly on previous empirical studies that predicted the relationship between the variables one intends to test at the current study. This means that you should have reviewed the literature before coming up with the hypothesis.

One formulates hypotheses by stating two hypotheses statements based on the research objective, the first statement is the one describes the expected relationship and the other which negates the expected relationship. In this case you state first how one variable is expected to relate to the other whether negatively or positively (Null Hypothesis). It doesn't matter which one starts but it will be followed by a statement that negates the relationship stated (Alternative Hypothesis) in the first place.

The Null hypothesis is represented by notation HO with an alternative hypothesis notation of HA

Example of Null Hypothesis

HO:1: There is a relationship between bank ownership structure and service quality in Tanzanian banks

Example of Alternative Hypothesis

HA:1: There is no relationship between bank ownership structure and service quality in Tanzanian banks

One should note that not all studies may require a formulated hypothesis. If research is inductive, where the study is just expected to be explanatory, it is unlikely to require a hypothesis. It is also possible that one research objective can have minor hypotheses which need to be tested in the study and in these instances, they may be stated after the major hypotheses.

7.19.1 *Characteristics of good hypotheses*

Good hypotheses will provide proper guidance for the study while a weak hypothesis might mislead the researcher in selecting the correct methodology of the study and hence obtain poor research results. For a hypothesis to be considered good, it should have, at the least:

- A stated relationship between research variables
- Is directional and therefore able to help the researcher predict the most likely relationship between the variables
- Testable with quantitative statistical testing techniques
- Is supported by pervious and current empirical literature

Box 7.3. Example of Hypothesis Formulation

Hypothesis 1 has been formulated to evaluate the relationship between bank ownership structure and service quality. However, Lynn, Lytle and Samo (2000) concluded that private banks outperform public banks in both service orientation and business performance. In respect to entry of private banks, Kangi and Kareklis (2001) argue that public and private banks behave and deal differently with their customers and employees though public banks are likely to be under control, more bureaucratic usually more honest and less concerned with profits. Entry of private banks has revolutionized the way in which banks depart from monopolistic banking operations to competitive operations. Sureshchandar et al. (2003) argue private banks kindle competitive spirit within public banks, but public banks are less concerned with quality services in relation to diversity and range of services offered. In this study the hypotheses are stated hereunder:

H 1: There is a relationship between bank ownership structure and Service Quality of Tanzanian banks

Hypothesis number one has another five minor hypotheses stated here under

- *H: 1a: There is a positive relationship between bank ownership and service quality in terms of tangibility*
- *H: 1b: There is a positive relationship between bank ownership and service quality in terms of reliability*
- *H: 1c: There is a positive relationship between bank ownership and service quality in terms of responsiveness*
- *H.1d: There is a positive relationship between bank ownership and service quality in terms of Assurance*
- *H.1e: There is a positive relationship between bank ownership and service quality in terms of Empathy*

Source: Yona 2016

7.19.2 Challenges commonly faced when formulating hypotheses

Students find the process of formulating the hypotheses of their studies challenging for various reasons. The following are some of the common challenges related to formulating the research hypotheses:

a. ***Unclear understanding of the type of study one is conducting*** and so confusion about what type of hypothesis is needed, if any;
b. ***Lacking empirical literature*** sufficient to support the expected prediction of the relationship between research variables;
c. ***Formulating Non-directional hypotheses***
d. ***Difficulty in differentiating and stating the null and alternative hypotheses***
e. ***Using the wrong notations for null and alternative hypotheses***
f. ***Hypotheses out of order (null and alternative)***

7.19.3 Testing of Research Hypothesis

Hypothesis testing tries to establish whether a particular claim is true or false by using different statistical techniques (Baradyana and Mwasele, 2000). There are different statistical techniques which students can use to test research hypotheses. The methods used depends completely on the nature of the study, the researcher's knowledge of the testing methods and his or her ability to analyze and explain results. The type of data collected will also influence the methods of testing the hypothesis.

The use of such as Chi-squared test, T-tests, F-Test, correlation analysis, regression analysis, T-tests, ANOVA, and MANOVA techniques can be appropriate in testing your hypotheses. It is not expected that all methods will be used in one study, but students should study a variety of techniques to determine what is most needed for their particular study.

The use of good statistical software such as SPPS or STATA can be very useful in data analysis especially when calculating correlations analyses and regression analyses particularly in quantitative research studies. The use of other packages such as NVivo can help one analyze qualitative data. The thesis should clearly state methods for testing one's research objectives from the proposal stage to the report writing stage. It is possible that the testing methods will not be the same from one research objective to another research objective. It will be useful to tabulate the research hypothesis and the testing method for each of the hypothesis.

7.20   Ethical Considerations in Research

Ethical considerations are another important aspect in the research process, especially when it comes to data collection, especially when human subjects are involved. Ethical consideration requires planning from the initial inception of the research design and the approval from respective ethical research committees.

Ethical consideration in research will include key issues such as ethical expectations, informed consent of participants, risk of harm, anonymity and confidentiality and avoidance of conflict of interest.

(i) **Ethical expectations:** Include ethical approvals, adherence to institutional regulations, use of specific ethics literature and designing ethical research approval

(ii) **Informed consent**: According to Fleming (2018), informed consent from all human participants means that all participants know:
- Who the researcher(s) are,
- What the intent of the research is,
- What data will be collected from participants,
- How the data will be collected from participants,
- What level of commitment is required from each participant?
- How collected data will be used and reported, and
- Any potential risks of taking part in the research.

(iii) **Anonymity**: This means non-disclosure of participants' identity except to the researcher

(iv) **Confidentiality:** This means participants' identity and information given by them should only be known to the researcher.

7.21   Organization of the Research Methodology Chapter

The research methodology chapter is a crucial chapter in thesis work. How one organizes the chapter will help readers understand how the research was carried out and how data were collected and analyzed. Therefore, it is important to adopt most acceptable formats for presenting this chapter in your thesis. The chapter must be organized in proper sections with each section explaining specific key issues of the methodology addressed. Normally, the research methodology should be discussed under Chapter 4 (assuming that the conceptual framework is discussed under Chapter 3). The following is the recommended order which one should follow to organize the research methodology chapter. The details which should be included in each of the following sections below have been discussed in the above sections

4.1 Introduction
4.2. Research Design
4.3. Study Population
4.4 Study Area
4.5 Sampling Method
4.6. Sample Size
4.7 Data Collection Methods
4.8 Data Analysis
4.9 Data Reliability and Validity
4.10. Research Hypothesis
4.11 Testing of Research Hypothesis
4.12 Ethical Considerations
4.13 Chapter Conclusions

7.22 Conclusions

This chapter on research methodology has tried to explain how research should be carried out by any researcher. It has provided proper explanations about how an individual can make choices about their study population, how to select and justify the study area and how to decide on a sampling method and sample size. The chapter also explains how an individual can collect and analyze the research data that can help the researcher to achieve the research objectives and answer the research questions. Additionally, this chapter has aimed to provide guidance on how to formulate research hypotheses and highlight the characteristics of good research hypotheses. At the same time, the topic explains briefly some challenges commonly faced by students when formulating research hypotheses. Lastly, the chapter provides general guideline on how to organize the research methodology chapter.

Data analysis is an integral part of thesis research development. Where data collected are not properly analyzed, it is impossible to derive correct information for presentation from the data. This chapter was dedicated to defining research analysis includes and to explaining the techniques employed in data analysis. The chapter further explained some of the tools used for data analysis, data presentation formats and challenges in data analysis. The chapter information on data analysis is not exhaustive by any means and so students are encouraged to seek additional resources as needed and desired to improve understanding.

Practice Questions

Question 1

Discuss common challenges experienced by students in analyzing research data.

Question 2

Discuss different methods of presenting qualitative and quantitative data.

Question 3

What factors should someone consider when selecting a statistical software for data analysis?

Question 4

Discuss the reasons and importance of data analysis in research work.

Question 5

Under what circumstances should one consider using bar graphs for data presentation?

Question 6

Discuss the differences between quantitative data analysis and qualitative data analysis.

Question 7

Discuss the qualities of a good research instrument.

Question 8

Explain the advantages and disadvantages of using questionnaires to gather research data.

Question 9

Discuss the differences between focus group discussions and interview as research instruments.

Question 10

What factors would you consider when choosing a research instrument?

CHAPTER 8

THE RESEARCH REPORT

8.1 Introduction

The research report is the final piece of your research work and is developed after the completion of all other pieces. A good report depends on the quality of the statement of the problem, research objectives, research questions, conceptual framework, types of data collected and research hypotheses. However, the report writing style, language and organization of the report are also of great importance as they will decide whether the thesis report will be accepted or rejected by the examining committee. Before submitting a report, students should seek assistance with editing from fluent English speakers to ensure that all spelling and grammar errors have been resolved. Students should also ensure that they meet the minimum requirements by the examining institutions in terms of minimum number of words and number of pages as these requirements will have a direct impact on if the student passes or fails.

8.2 The Thesis order

Theses need be organized in chapters. In this chapter, it is recommended that one writes the academic thesis in a specific order for which is accepted by most prestigious business schools worldwide. The standard order for thesis chapters is:

Abstract
Chapter 1: Introduction
Chapter 2: Literature Review
Chapter 3: Conceptual Framework
Chapter 4: Research Methodology
Chapter 5: Research Findings
Chapter 6: Conclusions and Recommendations
References
Appendices

Previous chapters have already outlined what is expected in regard to what should be written in each chapter, but the following sections are dedicated to providing information about how to write the abstract, research findings chapter (Chapter 5) and the final chapter (Chapter 6) on conclusions and recommendations. The abstract has to be written after the whole work has been finished.

8.3 Abstract

The way you write your abstract it should help someone to understand your thesis work that you have done for a longer and summarize the whole thesis report. The abstract page is expected to give a brief background of the study and summarize the details of the research work. It will state clearly the main research objective of the study as well as the specific objectives, the scope of the study, the methodology used for data collection and explain how data was analyzed. It has to be written in the past tense to show that the research is complete and not an ongoing work. The abstract should explain the major research findings of each research questions and show how research hypotheses were tested and their conclusions. The abstract chapter should also summarize the major findings of research as well the conclusions from the findings as well.

Box 8.1 Example- Sample of Abstract

Abstract

The dominant capital structure studies across the globe have been concentrated in developed countries and specifically for listed companies and few on unlisted companies or mixed companies. This thesis aims to examine the extent to which company liquidity, profitability, tangibility and company size influences the leverage of Tanzanian companies as suggested by Pecking Order and Trade off theory.

More specifically, this study adopts quantitative methods to analyze the extent to which liquidity, profitability, tangibility and company Size influences the leverage of Tanzanian companies. Panel data were collected from both listed and unlisted companies in Tanzania for period of seven years beginning 2007 to 2014.

The study findings show a negative relationship between company liquidity and company leverage as measured by debt ratio and debt to equity ratio. These findings show the validity of the pecking order theory in Tanzania. The postulates of the trade-off theory as far as liquidity is concerned are not valid. The study findings also reveal a positive relationship between profitability and leverage suggesting that majority of Tanzanian companies used more debts as the means of financing their business operations despite of their profitability. These findings are backed up with the existence of few companies that are listed in the stock exchange that are able to raise funds through equity funds.

The study found that the Tangibility of listed companies was higher than that of the unlisted companies and there was a negative relationship between Tangibility and leverage which is valid to Pecking order but contrary to trade off theory. This suggests that the majority of Tanzanian companies had adequate fixed assets for collateralization and hence allowed these companies to use debts as the means of financing their business operations. As far as company size is concerned study findings suggest that Pecking order theory (POT) and Trade off Theory (TOT) relevance cannot fully supported in Tanzanian companies as the findings have revealed a negative relationship between company size and leverage.

> Based on the findings on liquidity the study used only one variable to measure liquidity (Current ratio against two variables of dependent variable (debt ratio and debt equity ratio). Therefore, conducting a further research based on use of more variables indicators of liquidity and leverage could result into different findings and conclusions. Since the study did not establish the reasons for the decline in return on assets and return on equity for Tanzanian companies. Further research on what really influences profitability of Tanzania companies over time is needed in order to establish the causes of such major declines and develop strategies to enhance the company profitability. Further research study is needed to investigate what kind of Policies or strategies are needed in Tanzania to encourage more companies to access funding through equity.
>
> The study did not establish the relationship between short term assets tangibility and leverage of Tanzanian companies. This suggest that further studies could be necessary to understand the relationship between short term assets tangibility and leverage. The study did not confirm on the relationship of tangibility with other capital structure theories hence a suggestion for further study.
>
> As far as the relationship between company Size and Leverage the study used only one measures of company size namely log of Sales in this particular study. The use of different indictors of company size is likely to give different results hence a need for further research which might give different conclusions which may concur to the predictions of the pecking order and trade off theories.
>
> Source: Yona (2018) The Analysis of Factors influencing leverage of Tanzanian Companies

8.4   Research Findings Chapter

The research finding chapter is a critical chapter in your thesis. It will explain and summarize the findings of each of the research question and the hypotheses stated in the research. However, ensuring proper order of presentation matters, which information to start first and which to be presented at the end. It is important to remember that a good thesis report should ensure that all research questions are properly answered, research objectives are achieved, and conclusions of the research findings are made known. The research finding chapters are outlined and explained below.

8.4.1 Introduction

This section should provide a summary of what is expected from the research finding chapter. For example, *"This chapter describes research findings for all the research objectives of the study. Specifically, it gives detailed information on the demographic distribution of respondents, descriptive statistics of each of the research questions, hypothesis testing, discussion of each of the research findings and at the end it gives conclusions and recommendations"* (Yona 2016).

8.4.2 Demographic Information

This section should be dedicated to the summary of statistics of respondents to the research questionnaires in terms of age, sex, location, income groups etc. Questionnaires can either be structured or unstructured according to the data needed and as designed through different research instruments. The section should explain, in a simple form, the composition of the sample so that conclusions can be drawn from the study. Presentation of demographic information may be done by using tables, graphs or pie charts but with sufficient explanation.

8.4.3 Research Findings for Research Objectives

This section includes descriptive statistics of the findings related to each of your research questions, testing of the research hypotheses, discussion of the research findings and concluding comments. It is important since there are multiple research questions, that the questions be listed separately. For example, in a study by Yona (2016), "The Impact of Bank Ownership on Banking Competitiveness," the research finding section of the research question was stated as:

Box 8.2: Sample Research Findings

> Research Findings: The Impact of Bank ownership on Service Quality
>
> "This section presents the descriptive statistics, Overall performance of Individual service quality dimensions, Hypothesis Testing, Discussion, conclusions and recommendations. We state research question one (RQ1) here under "***To what extent bank ownership structure influences the banking competitiveness in terms of Service quality? The results are presented hereunder,***" Yona (2016).

Since there are more than one research questions in a thesis, after the discussion of the research findings and conclusion of the first research question you have to dedicate another section to show the findings of the other research questions in the same order as mentioned above.

Descriptive statistics

In the descriptive statistics section, one is expected to outline the inputs from responses of the questionnaires, focus groups discussions, primary data and other sources. Descriptive statistics are important in showing and summarizing data in a meaningful way even though it is not possible to make conclusions based on analyzed data. Descriptive statistics also do not help us to make a conclusion on the research hypotheses. Descriptive statistics are simply listed to describe and give more information about the data obtained.

Descriptive statistics can be presented by using tables, graphs and pie charts. The choices of presentation depend on the types of data gathered and the expected audience. Proper explanation of the tables, graphs and pie charts is important to give all readers a clear understanding of the data and information. There are two types of descriptive statistics which include measure of central tendency and measure of spread.

Measure of Central Tendency

The measure of central tendency is a single value that attempts to describe a set of data by identifying the central position within that set of data. As such, measures of central tendency are sometimes called measures of central location (In order to know when and how to use these kinds of measures you need to learn them in a statistical module. This book is not intended to teach you statistics but just to mention that measures of central tendency include the mean, mode and median. You should familiarize yourself with these statistical techniques. Knowing how to calculate them and interpret them is important.

Measure of Spread

Measures of spread are most commonly used in summarizing a group of data by describing how the scores depart or differ from the average scores of the group. Let say the average income of our 100 employees is $1,000 with a maximum income of $2,000. Not all employees will have an average income of $1,000 out of $2,000. Their income will be spread out, some with lower income and other with higher income. Therefore, measures of spread will help to explain or summarize how spread out these scores are. Measures of spread include the range, absolute deviation, variance and standard deviation.

Students need to understand how to calculate these measures and give proper interpterion and meaning to their audience. Sometimes students try to use these measures, but they fail to give proper interpretation of the data.

Example of Descriptive Statistics Presentation

As already mentioned above, the use of different measures, whether they are measure of spread or measure of central tendency to describe descriptive statistics depends on the type of data. The following are examples in presenting descriptive statistics of the previously mentioned study, "The Influence of Company Profitability on Leverage of Tanzanian Companies (Yona 2019).

Box 8.3: Example - Descriptive statistics

In this section we present the descriptive statistics on the company profitability of both listed and unlisted companies as well the hypothesis testing, discussion of the research findings consistency with previous studies and capital structure theories, conclusions and recommendations. We restate specific research question three here under, "To what extent company profitability influence the Leverage of Tanzanian Companies?". The results are presented hereunder:

5.1 Summary Statistics

According to table 4.17 various statistical indicators show the characteristics of profitability indicators by both listed and listed companies. In terms of profitability which is measured by return on equity (ROE), unlisted companies have higher mean of 4.89 and standard deviation of 26.09 with minimum and maximum value of -0.82 and 330.4 respectively in 213 observations. Listed companies have lower mean value of 0.54 and standard deviation of (26.09) with minimum and maximum value 0f – 0.16 and 2.72 respectively in 53 observations. These results mean that unlisted companies' shareholders were able to receive higher return for every single shilling invested as compared to listed companies. However, the minimum negative value by both companies means that some companies were making losses.

Table 4.17: Descriptive statistics of Return on Equity (ROE)

Variable	Listed Company	Unlisted Company
Mean	0.44	4.89
Median		
Standard Deviation	0.54	26.09
Minimum	-0.16	-0.82
Maximum	2.72	330
Observation	53	213

Source: Researcher 2017

On return on assets (ROA) the results (Table 4.18) show that unlisted companies have higher mean value of 1.37 and standard deviation of 10.28 in 212 observations with minimum and maximum value of -0.63 and 139.90 respectively. The listed companies had mean value of 0.23 and standard deviation of 0.3 in 53 observations with minimum and maximum value of -0.11 and 1.49 respectively. The negative minimum value of ROA is explained by company characteristics in the sample and signifies that some companies were operating in losses in some years. These results mean that unlisted companies assets generated more return than the assets by listed companies. Since ROA is assumed to be the measure of company's ability to generate capital internally (Kester 1986, Pandey et al 2000) these results show that unlisted companies generated more return internally than the listed companies.

Table 4.18: Descriptive statistics of Return on Assets (ROA)

Variable	Listed Company	Unlisted Company
Mean	0.23	1.37
Median		
Standard Deviation	0.3	10.28
Minimum	-0.11	-0.63
Maximum	1.49	139.90
Observation	53	213

Source: Researcher 2017

Descriptive statistics can also describe the responses of the sample's questionnaires. Consider the following examples from another study: **Bank Ownership Influence on Service Quality (Yona 2016).**

Box 8.4 Example 2- Descriptive Statistics

Findings on Research Question 1 This section presents the descriptive statistics, Overall performance of Individual service quality dimensions, Hypothesis Testing, Discussion, conclusions and recommendations. We state research question one (RQ1) here under, ***"To what extent bank ownership structure influences the banking competitiveness in terms of Service quality?"***. The results are presented hereunder:

4.3.1 Descriptive statistics

In order to answer the research question one and understand the relationship between bank ownership structure and service quality dimensions we first gave the findings on demographic characteristics above (Section 4.2.1) and then calculate the mean scores and standard deviation for each of the service quality variables namely tangibility reliability, responsiveness, assurance and empathy for two groups of banks namely private and semi-quasi banks. The questionnaires to customers adopted the SERVQUAL model of service quality to analyze customer perception of service quality as the result of financial sector reforms on bank ownership. (Q7- Q26). The results are presented in five sub-sections on each service dimension.

4.3.2. Responses of Customers on service Quality Dimensions

Responses on Tangibility

The statement dimension for tangibility asked for responses on four dimensions of tangibility. The first statement (Q7) asked for responses on whether a bank had updated equipment. The second and third questions asked whether banks' physical facilities were appealing (Q8), whether bank employees are well-dressed and appeared neat (Q9). The last question asked whether the appearance of the physical facilities of the Bank is in keeping with the type of services provided.

(Q10). The responses are presented in Table 4.2 below. According to the table below, a total of 70% (28%+42%) of bank customers from private banks as compared to those from semi or quasi banks 64% (22%+42%) disagreed that banks have up-to-date equipment. The results show that 74% (24%+50%) of private bank customers disagreed that banks have physical facilities that are appealing as compared to only 14% (13%+1%) who agreed on the statement and 11% were not sure. The responses from semi-quasi banks show that 58% (19%+39%) disagreed with the statement and only 7% agreed while 19% were not sure.

Table 4. 3 Customer Responses on Tangibility

Variable	Bank Ownership	Strongly Disagree	Disagree	Not Sure	Agree	Strongly Agree	Total
7. The bank has up to date Equipment	Private	60(28%)	88(42%)	32(15%)	25(12%)	6(3%)	211(100%)
	Semi Quasi	138(22%)	265(42%)	78(12%)	109(17%)	37(6%)	627(100%)
8. Bank Physical Facilities Appealing	Private	51(24%)	106(50%)	23(11%)	28(13%)	3(1%)	211(100%)
	Semi Quasi	122(19%)	246(39%)	96(15%)	117(19%)	46(7%)	627(100%)
9. Banks employees are well dressed and appear neat	Private	74(35%)	80(34%)	19(9%)	32(15%)	6(3%)	211(100%)
	Semi Quasi	203(32%)	231(37%)	39(6%)	95(15%)	59(9%)	627(100%)
10. The appearance of the physical facilities of the Bank is in keeping with the type of services provided.	Private	41(19%)	93(44%)	38(18%)	32(15%)	7(3%)	211 (100%)
	Semi Quasi	85(14%)	249(40%)	111 (18%)	125(20%)	55(9%)	627(100%)

Source:

8.4.4 Hypothesis Testing

In this section writers are expected to explain how hypotheses have been tested. The section will explain the methods used to test hypotheses such as the use of T-tests, correlation and regression analysis, but all depends on types of data you have. At the end and give conclusions of the testing.

It is advised to re-state the hypothesis first and then proceed with the testing and then give conclusions there-after to test all the research hypotheses. Hypothesis testing can also be supported by previous conclusions of similar hypotheses in the past. The following is the example of hypothesis testing from a previous study (Yona 2016).

Box 8.5 Example- Hypothesis testing

The first hypothesis is tested by using a t-test for testing for the existence of any significant relationship between bank ownership structure and various dimensions of service quality with the aim of understanding the relationship between bank ownership structure and service quality dimensions following the privatization of banks. We restate the hypothesis hereunder:

H1: There is a relationship between bank ownership structure and service quality of Tanzanian banks

This hypothesis is tested in conjunction with minor hypotheses H: 1a, H: 1b, H: 1c, H: 1d, and H: 1e

H1a: There is a significant relationship between bank ownership and service quality tangibility

The results for t-test for service quality dimension are presented under table 4.16. The t-test matrix given in the table below shows that there is a significant relationship between bank ownership structure and banks having up-to date equipment's (t (836) = -2.665, P=0.008) as p<0.05. There is also a significant relationship between bank ownership structure and banks having physical facilities that are appealing (t (-1.935), p=0.000) as p<0.05. There is no significant relationship between bank ownership and bank employees being well dressed and appearing neat (t (836) =-3.418, P=0.053) as p>0.05. Finally, there is a significant relationship between bank ownership and banks appearance of the physical facilities of banks being kept with the type of services provided. We can therefore conclude that there is a significant relationship between bank ownership structure and service quality in aspect of Tangibility and therefore reject the Null hypothesis (H0: 1a) and accept the alternative hypothesis (Ha: 1a) T-test results show a significance difference between private banks and semi-quasi banks in terms of banks having up-to –date equipment's. It also shows for significance difference in physical facilities, bank employees dressing and appearance as well significance in the physical facilities of banks being kept with the type of services provided. This supports the finding of the mean scores as semi-quasi banks have higher scores than private banks in all areas of services dimensions.

Table 4.16 Service Quality Tangibility Dimensions-T-test Results

Tangibility	t	df	P-Value
7. The bank has up to date equipment	-2.665	836	0.008
8. Bank physical facilities are visually appealing.	-4.107	836	0.000
9. Banks employees are well dressed and appear neat.	-1.935	836	0.053
10. The appearance of the physical facilities of the Bank is in keeping with the type of services provided.	-3.418	836	0.001

Source: Yona (2016)

8.4.5 Discussion of the Research Findings

This section outlines the research findings as related to the research questions through explanatory descriptive statistics and hypothesis testing. The discussion in this chapter should focus on actual findings on research questions and the linkage of those findings to the theories adopted by the study. Any theory that is chosen to guide a study should be directly linked to the findings of the study. The discussion should show whether the theories you adopted in your study have a relationship with the research findings. It is possible to see the departure of the findings from the theories adopted; therefore, it is important to reveal this clearly and state where possible the reasons for such departure.

The discussion also should show the relationship between the findings of the current study and the previous empirical studies with proper citations. If current studies agree or disagree with previous studies should be discussed. It is possible that the findings of your study to be different with the past studies. Therefore, where possible, researchers should establish the reasons for such differences. The discussion should also explain the conclusions derived from hypotheses testing too as this vital to this section. The following example is an example of research findings discussion on a study on the influence of liquidity on leverage of Tanzanian companies (Yona, 2019) and shows the discussions of the findings in relationship to the research question, research hypothesis and theory of Trade-off Theory.

Box 8.6 – Example -Discussion on Research Findings

4.4.3 Discussions on Research Findings

Research findings have revealed that there is negative relationship between liquidity and leverage among Tanzanian companies. Liquidity is negatively related to both debt to equity ratio (H2:2a) and debt ratio (H2:2b). The findings of this study suggest that majority of Tanzanian companies are small and seem to have inadequate liquidity to finance their business activities by using internal funds hence majority of them will have to opt to use more debts to finance their activities. It is also evident that in Tanzania there are few companies that have access to equity funds through listing as the conditions easily excludes those companies with lower liquidity.

The findings of this study do match with only few findings of the previous studies in other countries. Mahmood and Mansor (2008) studied the listed companies in Malaysia to understand the relationship between liquidity and company leverage and found that there was a negative relationship between liquidity and debt levels. Ahmad and Aris (2015) study of capital structure determinants in service industry in Bursa Malaysia indicated a significant negative impact of liquidity on leverage. Negative relationship between liquidity and leverage is consistent to the prediction of the pecking order. Pecking order predicts a negative relationship between liquidity and company leverage. The findings of this study are not consistent to the Trade-off theory which predicts a positive relationship between liquidity and leverage and are not consistent with other previous studies. Sibilkov (2009) investigation on the effect of liquid assets on capital structure found that liquidity was positively correlated to leverage. Olayinka (2011) study in Nigeria companies concluded that leverage and liquidity are positively correlated. Another study on capital structure by Khalay (2013) in Malaysian companies found that there is a significant positive relationship between liquidity ratios and leverage. These findings were consistent with the trade- off theory.

The study of Croatian's companies by Sarlija and Hare (2012) revealed that there are statistically significant relationships between liquidity and leverage ratios. However, the relationship between liquidity and long-term leverage was weaker than the relationship between liquidity and short-term leverage.

8.4.6 Conclusions of the research findings chapter

This section should give the conclusions of the research findings against the research objectives and questions. In this section the conclusion is not about the whole study but is restricted to only one of the research objectives and the hypotheses arising from a specific research question. You should be able discuss the conclusions of each research questions and each of the research hypothesis.

To ensure that you have good flow on this sections it is will be appropriate to have different paragraph dedicated for conclusions from research findings and hypothesis testing The conclusions in this section should be derived from the research findings and hypothesis testing, and not the citations of findings from previous studies. Students make mistakes of not giving appropriate conclusions based on their current studies which waters down their research. It has to show what really did you find after investigation is what really matters in this section.

8.5 Conclusions and Recommendations—The Final Chapter!

This is the last chapter of your thesis! How very exciting and how very important that you get it just right. The conclusions and recommendations chapter should explain the findings of one's entire study and give appropriate recommendations. However, the conclusions of the study should be related to the current study and not any other previous studies. Students make mistakes of making conclusions and giving recommendations not related to the study. The easy way is to make conclusions as per each research questions findings and make recommendations that have relation with the research findings and not otherwise.

8.6 Conclusion

This chapter has tried to give readers a snapshot of what a research report should contain and what should be explained in each of the sections in the chapter. By following the guidelines provided in this chapter, one can easily write the final report of their thesis without major difficulties and, thereafter, submit the report for review before the final defense.

Practice Questions

Question 1

What are the important issues that need to be explained in the discussion section dedicated to research findings?

Question 2

What are the appropriate issues that the conclusion and recommendations chapter of your thesis should include?

Question 3

What does hypothesis testing mean to you? Discuss what should be included in the hypothesis testing section of a thesis.

Question 4

What are descriptive statistics? How can one explain descriptive statistics in his or her research findings thesis chapter?

CHAPTER 9
WRITING YOUR REFERENCES

9.1 Introduction

This final chapter should give a summary of all references cited throughout the main text from beginning to end. Most of the time students prefer writing this chapter after the completion of their theses which often results in the omission of several reference. So as not to omit any citations in the reference chapters, it is important to extract references on a continuous basis from the main text as the thesis it is being written.

Students must also utilize an acceptable way of summarizing citations in an academically appropriate manner. The reference should be summarized according to the requirement of the school but should adhere to Harvard style, Turabian, APA, or another widely accepted citation style.

9.2 Contents of the References Chapter

Over time the authors have observed a number of errors which students make when completing the references chapter. It is important to understand what should or should not be included. Therefore, below is an outline of what should and should not be included:

   a. Firstly, include the most recent references, and skip old references. Currently, there is a lot of literature available especially with the support of online libraries and therefore it is unacceptable to use

citations in your main text with references from old books and journals.
b. Do not include any reference which is not cited in the main text. This is one of the challenges where students are tempted to put in this chapter references which have not been used anywhere in the document.
c. It is easy to skip the references of citations which appear in the main text. There is such possibility of skipping references when you consider doing the reference chapter after completion of your work instead of doing it on continuous basis as you keep updating your materials.done at the end. All citations should be picked in this chapter.
d. Make sure that you have adequate number of references. Few references show that the study is shallow
e. Ensure that there is proper arrangement of the references. References should be arranged alphabetically starting from the lowest alphabet to the largest alphabet.

9.3 Conclusion

This chapter is very brief. It has just tried to explain how the reference chapter has to be done, what should be included and what should be excluded as well. It has explained in detail the contents of the reference chapter. It recommends for best practices which students should adopt when finalizing this last chapter of their thesis.

Practice Questions

Question 1

Discuss why the referencing chapter is an important part of the thesis projects?

Question 2

What should the main contents of the reference chapter be?

Question 3

Discuss possible weaknesses that can lower the quality of the reference chapter.

CHAPTER 10
THESIS DEFENSE

10.1 Why do theses need to be defended?

The idea of defending the thesis originated because some students do not do their thesis research work themselves. They may engage others to do the work on their behalf for payment. The main objective of thesis defense is to test whether the student is the owner of the thesis. In a defense situation a student has to appear in front of panelist to present his research work.

The panelist will have to satisfy themselves that the student presenting the thesis is the one who really did the work and nobody else. In the world we live today individual use different means to make money. There are individuals who can use thesis writing for students as the means of making money. These individuals are capable of writing good thesis on the behalf of the students and charge them some money especially weak students and students with senior working position who are busy and have no time to conduct research work themselves. In the academic world these practices are not excuses not to do your thesis alone.

The panelist will use different strategies and ask questions that can help to get the assurance that really the student did the research work himself or herself. Students should also understand that panelists don't just look at the thesis document but reading between spoken words as you do your presentation.

10.2 Preparing for Defense

The defense requires you to prepare a Power Point presentation of your thesis work and present it to the panelist of learned professors who will listen to you and make professional judgments. You should bear in mind that you cannot present everything about your thesis in few Power Point slides.

The Power Point presentation should be no more than twenty slides which can be presented within fifteen minutes or twenty minutes. If you have so many presentations slide you will not be able to finish within a given time. You should therefore be smart to present the key issues of your research. The following are the key issues that you need to put in your presentation slides:

a. Topic
b. Introduction
c. Statement of the Problem
d. Research Objectives
e. Research Questions
f. Literature Review
g. Conceptual Framework
h. Research Methodology
i. Research Findings
j. Conclusions
k. Recommendation

10.3 Power Point Presentation

The following are the sample of power point presentations slides for a doctorate degree in Business Administration (DBA) which was presented by the author at MsM. ***The thesis entitled "The Impact of Bank Ownership on Banking Competitiveness"*** You can use the format of these slides to suit your own defense presentation at master's level or doctorate level.

First Slide:

The first slide shows the title of the research, the researcher's name, names of the research supervisors as well as the name of panelists if known. This slide should not be clouded with too many words. All slides should be visible with clear and friendly colors.

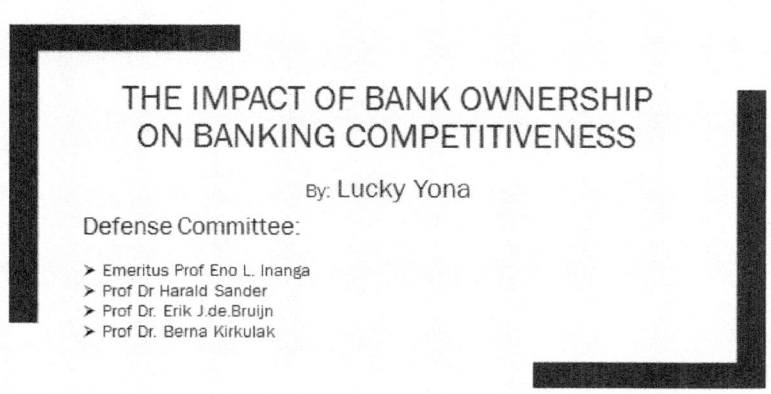

Second slide

This is should give the introduction. The second slide should give a brief historical background of the problem. It has to be in summary in forms in bullets format that you can easily explain them in detail before stating the problem statement of the research. Avoid putting too much information on the background of the study in one slide. Since you are the researcher, you are likely to have the information in your fingertips and should be able to give proper explanation easily on your defense.

Introduction

Prior to Financial Sector Reforms	Financial Sector Reforms
• Monopolistic characteristics of bank ownership (State) • Poor performance of Financial sector including the banks (Service Quality, Growth, profitability, Higher interest rates) • Reasons for poor performances (lack of competition, poor supervision, poor management, etc) • Need for reforms to reverse the situation	• Tanzania undertook variety of reforms (1990's) e.g. *interest rate liberalization, regulations, governance and Management*) • Bank ownership reforms was one of the reforms. • Objectives of the reforms (*Improve competitiveness of Banks*) Expectation from the reforms: • improved service quality and delivery, profitability, efficiency and effectiveness of the banks.

RESEARCH PROBLEM

Despite of the expected reforms in bank ownership there is inadequate studies/literature to show the influence of bank ownership on banking competitiveness in Tanzania (service quality, growth, efficiency and profitability)

Third Slide

The third slide should be used to summarize the research objectives and research questions. Both main research objectives and specific can be summarized in one slide. Condensing these in one slide is that it will help you to save your time and during the presentation you might opt to use only research objectives or research questions.

Research Objectives	Research Questions
Main Research Objective To Establish the influence of bank ownership structure on the banking competitiveness of commercial banks in Tanzania	**Major Research Question:** What is the influence of bank ownership structure on the banking competitiveness of Tanzanian commercial banks?
Specific research Objectives 1. To determine the extent to which bank ownership structure has influenced the service quality of Tanzanian commercial banks.	**Specific Research Questions** 1. To what extent does bank ownership structure affect the service quality of Tanzanian commercial banks
2. To assess the extent to which bank ownership structure influenced the growth of the commercial banks	2. To what extent does bank ownership structure affect the growth of the Tanzanian commercial banks?
3. To find out whether bank profitability and financial soundness is affected by bank ownership	3. To what extent does bank ownership structure affect profitability and financial soundness of Tanzanian commercial banks?
4. To determine the extent to which bank ownership structure influence efficiency in bank operations.	4. To what extent does bank ownership structure affect the efficiency of Tanzanian commercial banks

Source: Researcher 2016

Fourth Slide: Literature Review

The slide should summarize the key literature discussed under the literature review chapter. You have to group your sections and give citation of the papers cited only. You are not expected to discuss the whole literature at this juncture but highlighting the key issues or topics in the literature and few citations where necessary.

Source: Researcher (2016)

Fifth Slide: Conceptual Framework

The slide should give the diagrammatical representation of the conceptual framework. Show the independent variable as well as the dependent variable and label the diagram as well as the source.

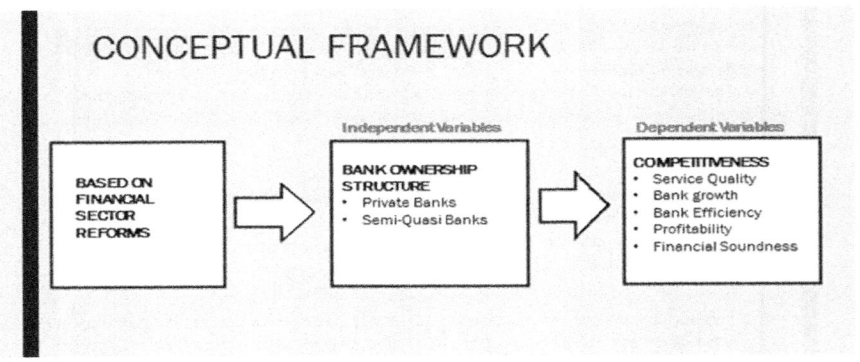

Source: Researcher 2016

Sixth and Seventh Slides

The number of slides is determined by the number of dependent variables. The study had five dependent variables to measures and two slides were dedicated to explain the proxy measurements (Slide six and seven) The slides should give a brief summary on how you will measure the variables and you should be able to define and explain them to the team of panelist. You need to show the panelist how each variable will be measured even if you are not able to explain them. This study had more than one dependent variable and hence two slides were used to show and explain how each variable was measured.

Proxy Measurement: Dependent Variables

Variable	Measurement
Service Quality (SERVQUAL MODEL)	**Tangibility** (*Physical appearance of facilities, employees appearance*) **Responsiveness** (*Prompt services, prompt responses to customers, willingness to help customers*) **Reliability** (*Keeping promises, providing dependable services etc*) **Assurance** (*Ability, competence and credibility of the bank to provide assurance to bank customers*) **Empathy** (*Caring, understanding customers, providing individual attention, communication*)
Bank Growth	**Quantitative Indicators** Size of Assets, Revenue, number of branches, customer base, level of lending, level of deposits, number of employees, market share **Qualitative Indicators** • Services extension to remote areas • Ability to manage Operational Costs efficiently
Efficiency	Operating Efficiency (*Efficient in terms of loans given against the cost of giving the loan*) Staff Income to staff Portfolio (Net Income each staff earned) Earning Per Staff (Measure of staff Productivity, Staff contribution to profitability)

Source: Yona 2016

Proxy Measurement: Dependent Variables (continued)

Variable	Measurement
Profitability	Return on Average Total Assets (ROAA), Return on Equity (ROE), Interest Income to Total Income, Earning Assets to Total Assets, Net Interest Margin
Financial Soundness	Capital Adequacy (Liquidity of Banks), Non Performing Loans to Gross Loans and Advances, Total Capital to Risk Weighted Assets (RWA,s), Liquid Assets to Total Assets (Current ratio) – Bank Liquidity

Eighth and Ninth Slides

The eighth and ninth slides can summarize the main research hypotheses together with the minor hypotheses of the study. In this example there were numerous hypotheses so two slides were required. Other studies may only require one slide for this information.

Research Hypotheses

Main Hypothesis	Minor Hypothesis
H1: There is a relationship between bank ownership and service Quality of Tanzanian Banks	Ho: 1a- Bank Ownership Vs Tangibility Ho: 1b- Bank ownership Vs Reliability Ho: 1c- Bank Ownership Vs Responsiveness Ho: 1d- Bank ownership Vs Assurance Ho: 1e- Bank ownership Vs Empathy
H2: Bank ownership structure is positively related to bank growth in Tanzania	Ho: 2a- Extension of services Ho: 2b- Increased number of customers Ho: 2c- Market Share Ho: 2d- Number of Staff Ho: 2e- Increased bank customer deposit Ho: 2f- Increased customer loans Ho: 2g- bank total assets
H3: Bank ownership is related to bank profitability of Tanzanian Commercial Banks	Ho: 3a- Bank Ownership Vs ROA Ho: 3b- Bank Ownership Vs ROE Ho: 3c- Bank Ownership Vs NIM Ho: 3d- Bank Ownership Vs Earnings to Total Assets Ho: 3e- Bank Ownership Vs Expenses to Interest Income

Source: Researcher 2016

Research Hypotheses (continued)

Main Hypothesis	Minor Hypothesis
H4: There is a relationship between bank ownership structure and financial Soundness of Tanzanian Banks	Ho:4a : Capital Adequacy Ho:4b : Non – performing loans to Gross loan, Ho:4c : Total Capital to Risk Weighted Assets Ho:4d : Core Capital to RWA, Ho:4e : Liquid Assets to Total Assets Ho 4f: Liquid assets to Deposit Liabilities
H5: There is a relationship between bank ownership and efficiency of Tanzanian Banks	Ho:5a : Operating Efficiency Ho:5b : Portfolio Yield Ho:5c : Staff Income to Staff Portfolio Ratio Ho:5d: Bank Average Loan Portfolio Ho:5e : Bank earning Capacity per staff

Source: Researcher 2016

Tenth Slide

This slide summarizes the methodology of your study such as the research design, study population, sampling method, sample size, data reliability, data validity, data analysis and research hypothesis.

Research Methodology

Research Design	A Case study (32 Banks operating in Tanzania by 2011) 4 Regions in Tanzania (Dar , Kilimanjaro, Arusha, Mwanza:)
Study Population	Commercial Banks (already Registered by BOT by end of 2011): Number of banks were below 50 : All 32 banks were considered (Small sample)
Sampling Method and Sample Size	Stratified Random Sampling: Customer – Sample 1,600 Bank Officials 224
Data Collection	Primary Data: Questionnaire's to walk in customers (836/1600), Questionnaire's to bank officials(81/224) Interview to Bank Officials (32) Secondary Data: Panel Data from Financial Statements (32 Banks) for period of six years (2006-2011)
Data Reliability and Validity	Crobach Alpha Coefficient (RQ1 and RQ 4) and Factor Analysis (Rq1 and Rq4)
Data Analysis and Hypothesis Testing	Rq1- Mean scores, standard deviation, t-tests - Service Quality dimensions Rq2. Mean Scores, Standard Deviation, t-Tests , Regression (Growth indicators) RQ3- Mean Scores, Standard Deviation, t-Tests , (Profitability and FS) RQ4- Mean Scores, Standard Deviation, Trend Analsyis, t-test (Efficiency

Source: 2016

Eleventh to Fourteenth Slides

The research findings of the study need to be given high importance and therefore even three or four slides may be used to summarize the major findings of the research along with conclusions and recommendations. One suggestion could be to use one slide for each of the tasks here: summarize the findings, conclusions and recommendation for each research objective and research hypothesis. However, this is only a suggestion and slides can be arranged in any way to best present the information.

Major Findings

H1: There is a relationship between bank ownership and service quality of Tanzanian Banks
Tested together with Minor Hypotheses (Ho:1a, Ho:1b, Ho:1c, Ho:1d, Ho:1e)

MAJOR FINDINGS	RECOMMENDATIONS
1. No Relationship: (Reliability, Assurance and Empathy). There is a Relation ship (Tangibility and Responsiveness)	1. Banks should pay closer attention to all service quality dimensions which customers scored them lowly.
2. No Significance difference: btw Banks in service quality dimensions	2. Banks should give priority in acquiring up-date equipment and improve their physical facilities
3. Non-significant not Equality: Private banks are more competitive in service quality than the semi-quasi banks	3. Banks staff should be sympathetic to their customers' needs, keep promises to their customers and provide services on time in order to increase service quality in terms of reliability.
4. Other factors are likely to explain the differences in service quality: (working culture of banks employee, Less attention on training, High staff turnover among banks and Increased fraud cases)	4. Banks should design customers focused policies and deliver quality services to meet customers' expectations
CONCLUSIONS	
Private banks are likely to be more competitive in service quality tangibility, Reliability, and Assurance, responsiveness	5. Banks should offer unique products that can address customers' needs

H2: Bank ownership is positively related to Bank Growth in Tanzania
Tested together with these minor Hypotheses (Ho:2a, Ho:2b Ho:2c, Ho: 2d, Ho:2e ,Ho:2f, Ho:2g)

MAJOR FINDINGS
1. There is No Relationship: Ho:2a – Extension of services; Ho:2b –Increased number of customers, Ho:2c-Market Share, Ho:2d-Number of Staff:
2. There is a Relationship: Ho: 2e- Increased bank customer deposit, Ho: Ho:2f- Increased customer loans, Ho:2g- Increased bank total assets
3. There is significant differences among banks in terms of growth indicators.

Conclusions
1. Semi Quasi banks have extended more services to remote areas, increased market share, increased number of staff, increased customer deposits, total assets and loan advances
2. Bank growth is also influenced by other factors e.g. size of banks on total assets, strategic plan of the banks to grow their balance sheet Knowledge of customers on usage of bank services

Recommendations
1. Government Support: the Private banks to extend their services to remote areas, support banks by depositing and channeling government funds through the commercial banks 2. Public Education on the importance of using bank services
2. Gov. policies that encourage the growth of economic activities and attraction of more foreign investors

H3: Bank ownership is related to bank profitability of Tanzanian Commercial Banks
Tested together with other Minor Hypotheses(Ho:3a, Ho:3b, Ho:3c, Ho: 3d)

MAJOR FINDINGS
1. There is no relationship between bank ownership structure and bank profitability [Ho: 3a : ROA Ho: 3b : ROE Ho: 3c : NIM Ho: 3d : Earnings to Total Assets Ho: 3e : Expenses to Interest Income]
2. There is no significance differences between banks in terms of profitability indicators

Conclusions
1. Private banks have higher scores in all profitability indicators (Except ROE) than semi-quasi hence more competitive than semi-quasi banks
2. The difference in profitability indicators not explained by bank ownership

Recommendations
1. Banks should Investigate on other factors that are likely to influence bank profitability other than bank ownership in order to enhance competitiveness

H4: There is a relationship between bank ownership structure and financial Soundness of Tanzanian Banks
Tested together with other minor Hypotheses (Ho: 4a, Ho:4b, Ho:4c, Ho:4d, Ho:4e, Ho:4f)

MAJOR FINDINGS
1. There is no relationship between bank ownership structure and financial soundness.
   [Ho: 4a : Capital Adequacy Ho: 4b : Non – performing loans to Gross loan]
   [Ho: 4c : Total Capital to Risk Weighted Assets Ho: 4d : Core Capital to RWA]
   [Ho: 4e : Liquid Assets to Total Assets]
   [Ho 4f: Liquid assets to Deposit Liabilities]
2. There is no significance differences between banks in terms of financial soundness

Conclusions
1. Private banks have higher mean scores than semi-quasi banks for almost all financial soundness indicators,
2. The variations are not explained by the type of bank ownership.

Recommendations
1. Banks should investigate on other factors that are likely to influence financial soundness other than bank ownership in order to enhance competitiveness

H5: There is a relationship between bank ownership structure and economic efficiency of Tanzanian banks
Tested together with Minor Hypotheses (Ho:5a, Ho:5b, Ho:5c, Ho:5d)

MAJOR FINDINGS	CONCLUSIONS
1. There is no significant relationship between bank ownership structure and banks efficiency indicators 2. There is no significance difference in bank efficiency indicators between semi-quasi and private banks **Recommendations** Banks should investigate on other factors that might have caused the changes of these bank efficiency variables over time as indicated in the trend analysis Note : Efficiency indicators Ho: 5a : Operating Efficiency Ho:5b : Portfolio Yield Ho:5c : Staff Income to Staff Portfolio Ratio Ho:5d : Bank Average Loan Portfolio Ho: 5e : Earning Capacity per staff	1. Private banks are more likely to have adequate operating hours convenient to customers and deal in transparency with customers. 2. Private banks more likely to have proper and accurate disclosers of f/statements 3. Semi-quasi banks are more likely to have adequate number of staff to deliver services 4. Private banks have higher scores in Quantitative indicators

Last Slide

The last slide can be used to summarize recommendations for further research directions. It is not necessarily to follow the exact number of slides outlined here and, in fact, it is recommended that you use the fewest number of slides necessary to present your thesis in a clear and effective way.

Further Research Direction

	Research Direction
Overall Research Direction	a. This research concentrated to only to individual customers and not corporate customers. A further study that incorporates corporate customers might reveal different results. b. Extension of further studies in other cities in the country could give different results c. Further impact studies on other areas of financial sector reforms that are likely to influence banking competitiveness
Service Quality	Study on what really influences service quality of banks in Tanzania other than bank ownership
Bank Growth	Study on what really can influence the growth of banks in Tanzania other than bank ownership
Profitability and Financial Soundness	Investigate the causes for different performances of the banks in terms of Profitability's and financial soundness
Efficiency	Further research on other factors than bank ownership that are likely to influence the efficiency of banks

Apart from preparing power point presentation, during presentation time you should note the following issues

(a) Dress smart during presentation. Avoid casual dress during presentation as this will reflect what type of the person you are. Avoid casual dress as this is important stage of in your academic career and therefore you need to be smart
(b) Since you have less time to present your work do not spend a lot of time on one slide. It is good to practice your presentation by using a clock so that you can know in advance if you are able to present the slides within the minimum required time.
(c) Do not read the slides when presenting your work. You have to address the supervisor and not reading the slides for them. Reading the slides will force you to show your back to the panelist who might make them angry and uninterested to listen to you. The panel members normally are happy to look at you and listen when presenting your work.

10.4 Conclusion

This chapter was dedicated to providing practical guidance on how students are expected to approach their defense session after thesis submission. The chapter has explained why it is important for a researcher to defend his findings, how he or she should prepare for thesis defense, what issues an individual should avoid during the defense session and the qualities of a good defense.

Practice Questions

Question 1

Why is defending a thesis an important stage in the research process?

Question 2

How should someone prepare for a thesis defense?

Question 3

What are the critical issues one should avoid during the defense session?

Question 4

What are qualities of a good defense which should be utilized during the thesis defense?

CHAPTER 11
PUBLISHING YOUR THESIS

11.1 Introduction

Over years of my work I have come to an understanding that the majority of students doing their master's degrees have not published their theses. Their valuable work has remained on their personal shelves at their educational institution and therefore has not added any value to the academic world and the community. There are many explanations to these practices. One reason being the lack of understanding by students on how to go about the process of publishing an academic paper or a book. The other reason for non-publication at the master's level is that publication is not a mandatory for getting a master's degree in most African universities. Only a few universities insist on paper publication before graduation and therefore many students simply never publish their thesis.

There are many opportunities that arise when one publishes their thesis. One of the advantages is that it gives the student an opportunity for his or her work to be known to policy makers who make policy decisions at the national and global level to use the findings of your research. One's contribution to the academic world is also enhanced and it may lead to a promotion at work. In the academic world, publication is life as per the common saying "Publish or Perish".

11.2 Converting a thesis into Publishable Paper

Converting your thesis into publishable paper is an art that requires you to summarize your thesis which has many pages into few pages that can be published in a journal. You should understand that each journal has it is own requirement on how you should submit your paper for review and once accepted it can be published. In any case the contents of the paper will not exclude the following key issues

a. Topic
b. Introduction
c. Statement of the Problem
d. Research Objectives
e. Research Questions
f. Literature Review
g. Conceptual Framework
h. Research Methodology
i. Research Findings
j. Conclusions
k. Recommendations
l. References
m. Appendices

The length of the paper depends so much on the requirements of the journal itself. Some journals do not accept papers with more than 15 pages and majority have a maximum limit of 25 pages. This means that researchers must summarize their work in such a way that one meets the requirements of the journal without watering down the contents of the research itself. At the master's level, one can publish one paper because but for a doctoral study more than one paper is likely needed.

At PhD level, since studies are very detailed, a smart student may publish three or more papers. The findings from each research objective and research question can converted into a publishable paper. Speaking from experience, while doing my doctorate degree I managed to produce four scientific papers which were published in high reputable journals (Yona 2017: Yona 2016: Yona 2015: Yona 2014). Your literature review will also be restricted to meet the research objectives.

It is also important when trying to write a research paper for publication to get input from your supervisor. In the academic world, your supervisor is the co-author of the paper and that should be acknowledged. His or her comments or contribution should be taken into consideration when writing the paper.

Condensing your literature review to contain the relevant key issues of the paper is important as the literature discussed in the whole thesis is too huge to be contained in a research paper. Ensure that there is proper citation in the literature as per journal requirements. The citations should not be omitted in the references sections neither you shouldn't include any citation in reference chapter which you haven't used it in the main document. Some thesis may have too many tables and graphs in the research finding chapters. Putting all the tables in a summarized paper may not be possible as the required pages are few. Therefore, the best way is to combine some tables into one table for examples the tables relating to demographic information and attaching few tables as appendices rather than putting them in main text.

11.3 Submitting your paper for journal publication

It is advisable that you submit your manuscript to a journal of your preference. that relates to the subject matter for publication consideration. However, each journal that you pick has its own guidelines that you have to meet before they accept your paper for publications. Some journals have high global ranking and would require high quality standards. They also exercise peer review and high-quality editorial, which means that you need to have adequate preparations to meet the required standards. The use of correct format on presentation of your paper matters a lot for consideration for publications. You have to ensure checking for spelling and grammatical errors. It is also important to note that each journal will have its own requirements and specific formats of presentation. Compliance to the requirements of the specific journal you want to publish in is of paramount importance.

In academia, published papers are subjected to peer review by other professionals in the area of study in order to obtain authentication on the quality and relevance of the paper. Majority of international journals will subject the papers submitted by authors to two or three independent people to review the papers before the paper is published. The outcomes from the decisions of the independent reviewer is critical for publication. Three options normally given by the reviewer are to accept the paper for publication with minor changes or reject the paper. In case the journal accepts your paper, it may issue an official letter of acceptance. Official acceptance letter is good for the author to show to academic employers in case where the paper has not yet been published. The following is the sample of a journal letter of acceptance:

11.4   Incorporating Reviewer Comments

Reviewers' comments for improvement on an article are given to help the writer determine if their piece is publishable or not and, if not, to inform needed improvements. In most cases a journal is willing to publish a paper upon incorporating their comments into a writers' original paper. It is rare for a journal to accept a paper without requiring the author to make some changes and these are changes are explained in the reviewers' reports.

Most journals will give a time limit for incorporating their recommendations before the paper's publication. Since there are likely many authors who want to publish their articles in the same journal, it is important to comply with their requirements and ensure that the reviewers' comments are incorporated into one's writing within the set timeline.

The comments might involve grammatical or spelling checks, improvement on the literature review, linking your research findings with conclusions and improvement on the discussions of the research findings as well as making sure of proper citation and referencing.

11.5   Converting a thesis to a book

A thesis is initially prepared for academic purposes which lead to obtaining a degree but might not be relevant for broader audiences. However, most theses can also be published as books to benefit others with a few changes. Converting a thesis into a book requires an understanding of the book's target audience and how the audience will benefit from the book. Writers need to ask themselves the following questions before taking any steps towards completing their thesis to book conversion:

A. Are your research findings and literature review valuable to broader audiences?
B. Does the research cover topics of interest to broader audiences? If not, the book will sit unread outside of academia. Does the scope of the research meet the interest of readers globally?
C. How feasible is it in converting the thesis structure to book structure?
D. Who will be willing to read and buy the book anyway?

The answers to these questions will help writers decide whether the transition of thesis to book is feasible and useful.

If the book is intended to benefit those who are doing a thesis at doctorate level or master's level, one may decide to publish the whole thesis without any removal or may decide to publish a series of short books highlighting different sections of the thesis.

11.6 Conclusion

This chapter has provided guidance on how an individual can modify his or her thesis into a publishable book or article from the thesis for publication in a peer reviewed journal. The chapter has briefly highlighted the major contents of issues that need to be included in any paper publication in the journal and explained the requirements needs to be fulfilled before publishes his or her paper.

Practice Questions

Question 1

Why is it important to publish your thesis?

Question 2

What are the pre-requisite requirements for publication of journal papers?

Question 3

Discuss how one can go about converting his/her thesis into a book.

APPENDIX

APPENDIX 1: SAMPLE PUBLISHED PAPER 1

Tax System and Small Business Compliance: The Case of the Republic of Seychelles

Emmaline Camille [1*] Lucky Yona[2]

1. Seychelles Revenue Commission, Maison Collet, Victoria, Mahé, Seychelles
2. Eastern and Southern African Management Institute P.O Box 3030, Arusha, Tanzania

Abstract

The purpose of this study was to identify whether the tax system is influencing the level of small business compliance with tax laws in the Republic of Seychelles. Four variables were identified under the tax system, namely the tax rates, record keeping, tax audits and tax penalties. 360 small businesses from twelve different sectors were randomly selected to take part in this study through self-administered questionnaires. The SPSS 20.0 was used to test the strength of the relationship between the tax system and compliance levels, using the Pearson Correlation Coefficient method. The results proved that the tax rates, record keeping, tax audits and tax penalties all have a strong positive relationship with tax compliance. This implies that improvement in these variables will surely lead to improved compliance amongst small businesses.

Keywords: Seychelles tax system, small business tax compliance

1. Introduction

Governments all over the world have the responsibility of providing various public goods and services to their citizens. As a result, governments incur significant expenses on behalf of their citizens to ensure that their basic needs are being met. Since a huge sum of funds is required to do this, governments have to identify sources of funding, and one of these is through the collection of taxes. Modugu and Anyaduba (2014) define a tax as "…a compulsory levy imposed by the government on the income, profit or wealth of an individual, family, community corporate or unincorporated bodies etc. for purposes of financing public expenditures". The government exercises its powers to collect revenue through taxation legislation, which are usually performed through a Revenue Authority. According to the Organization for Economic Co-operation and Development (OECD, 2014), one of the main objectives of any Revenue Authority is to ensure that the Government is collecting taxes and duties payable in a fair and effective way, and at the same time ensuring that taxpayers maintain their trust in the revenue administration system. OECD (2014) explains that it is important for revenue authorities to ensure that the level of compliance in their respective country is high so that the country can maximize the level of revenue that is collected from taxpayers. According to Abdi (2010), tax compliance is when taxpayers abides to all tax laws and regulations and fulfill their obligations such as lodging their returns on time and paying their fair share of taxes due.

In the Republic of Seychelles, the system of self-assessment has been adopted. According to Kwai Fatt and Wong Sek Khin (2012), this is a system whereby taxpayers are responsible for calculating and reporting their tax due to the revenue authority. The revenue authority on the other hand has to ensure that taxpayers are making an honest declaration of their tax liabilities by investigating whether they are complying with tax laws, which is usually done through tax audits and enforcement activities. It can be argued that this system fosters voluntary compliance, but only if the authority has an effective system of auditing, and efficient compliance and enforcement activities. In the case of the Seychelles Revenue Commission (SRC), these units are very small and lack the required human resource capacity to perform their duties effectively, thus leaving taxpayers with the possibility of being non-compliant without being detected.

Non-compliance may be the result of taxpayers' actions such as their own negligence, lack of knowledge, intentional tax evasion or could even be the underperformance of a tax authority in fulfilling its duties effectively. They are responsible for ensuring that all taxpayers abide to the revenue laws and understand and meet their tax obligations. According to the SRC's Taxpayers Charter (2012), the obligations of taxpayers are as follows: To register as a taxpayer, submit tax returns and pay the right amount of tax on time, inform SRC of significant changes in the business, to notify SRC of any mistakes made on the returns, provide auditors with the appropriate information to conduct effective auditing. And lodge objections / appeals within the timeframe. The

Ministry of Finance, Trade and Investment introduced a new tax, falling under the normal Business Tax for small businesses to pay. The Presumptive Tax came in force in January 2013 and was designed for small businesses earning an annual turnover of less than SR 1 million per year. The Presumptive Tax removes all other obligations from the small businesses, including the Value Added Tax (VAT) and the Business Tax. Other than the Presumptive Tax, small businesses are liable to pay only their Income and Non-Monetary Benefits Tax (INMBT). The change was done to make it easier and cheaper for small businesses to meet their tax obligations. The Presumptive Tax Return is a one page document that is simple and easy to complete, compared to the Business Tax Return, where small businesses had to acquire the expertise of tax agents to complete their forms. However, regardless of the simplification that was done by the MOFTI, compliance rate has still not yet gone up to the desired level.

2. Statement of the problem

The International Finance Corporation (2007) explains that small businesses are key contributors to most economies globally. In the case of the republic of Seychelles, there are 14,222 businesses registered with the SRC (SRC Annual Report, 2014). Out of this, 3223 are registered under the small business regime. This represents 22.66% of the total number of businesses registered with the SRC. However, although the proportion of small businesses is quite significant, the amount of taxes collected from this category is only 0.1% of the total amount of revenue collected. The SRC recorded a total of SCR 1.5 billion from all tax collections, and small businesses only contributed SCR 6,846,000 (SRC Annual Report, 2014). This could be an indication that small businesses are not being fully compliant with tax laws. Small businesses not complying with tax laws means that returns are lodged late, payment is overdue, businesses are evading taxes by keeping records from audit officers, and other sorts of non-compliant behavior.

The collection of taxes has been one of the main topics in the media in the past few years. Since the beginning of the economic reform in 2008, the citizens of Seychelles have been questioning the works of the revenue authority. According to Vadde and Gundarapu (2012), one of the main problems faced by revenue authorities is the lack of officers to conduct audits and inspect whether taxpayers are complying with tax laws. This is of no exception to the Republic of Seychelles. There are a total of 14,222 businesses that have been registered with the SRC, and there are a total of only 26 officers in the Audit Unit. Table 1 indicates the number of officers allocated to each Audit Unit according to the size of businesses.

Table 1: Number of Audit Officers in each Audit Unit

Audit Unit	Number of SRC Officers
Large Business Unit	12
Medium Business Unit	9
Small Business Unit	5

Source: SRC Human Resources Division

Catching tax evaders is no easy job when facing serious lack of resources to complete the tasks. This has led to an increase in the level of non-compliant businesses, since first of all, tax payments are based on self-assessment, and secondly, taxpayers are aware that the probability of being audited is quite low. According to the Small Audit Unit Manager, only 94 audits of small businesses were conducted in the year 2014. This represents only 3% of the total number of small businesses.

According to the SRC (2014) database, the compliance rate for the year 2014 was only 33%, therefore implying that there is an urgent need to identify why some taxpayers are not compliant. The table below indicates the general rates of compliance for all business since 2010. The SRC database also recorded 1485 businesses that lodged their 2014 tax return late. This represents 46% of businesses not submitting their return on time.

Table 2: Compliance rates for 2010 to 2014.

2010	2011	2012	2013	2014
54%	45%	43%	44%	33%

Source: SRC Database

The compliance rates are alarmingly decreasing over the years, thus there is a need to identify the root cause of the problem. The most common form of non-compliance identified was late lodgment and payment of taxes due, followed by tax evasion. This is when taxpayers intentionally escape taxes for example, by declaring false income to the revenue authority. The possible reasons underlying the act of being non-compliant is what will be discussed in this study. Further investigation is required to first of all identify why small business are not making a significant contribution and secondly, why they are not complying with their tax obligations.

3. Literature review

3.1 Tax Systems

The IMF, OECD and the World Bank (2011) explain that turning a tax system into one that is simpler, more equitable and transparent remains a challenge for most developing countries. The authors further argue that an effective tax system is the key to organizing and mobilizing the country's resources to achieve economic growth. It becomes the responsibility of the tax administration to ensure that an effective and efficient tax system is in place, yet it remains one of most common challenges for many revenue authorities across the globe. A weak tax system has proven by studies conducted by Lignier and Evans (2012), Gambo et al (2014) and Nurlis (2015) to be one of the main causes of non-compliance with tax laws. Some features of a weak tax system include no integrated approach to different taxes, unfair tax laws, poor service delivery, poor governance and the presence of corruption.

3.2 Small Business and Tax Compliance

IMF (2015) defines tax compliance as "meeting all obligations imposed by the tax system". Mas'ud et al (2014) explain that there are two forms of compliance. The first one is administrative compliance, whereby taxpayers abide to tax laws and regulations, and secondly there is judicious compliance, which is the accuracy of information entered in tax returns. The authors further mention that compliance can be achieved either voluntarily by taxpayers or through enforcement activities by relevant authorities. According to Batrancea et al (2012), the Economic Theory of Tax Compliance developed by Allingham, Sandmo (1972) and Srinivasan (1973) helps in understanding some factors that will influence the level of compliance. The theory is based on three deterrent variables, namely tax rate, tax audit and probability of being detected. This theory suggests that that businesses are likely to evade taxes if the tax rates are high and probability of being audited and detected are low.

Lignier and Evans (2012) explain that complying with tax laws can have significant costs to small businesses. These would include the cost of the taxes themselves, administrative costs of computing and calculating their taxes or cost of hiring a tax agent / accountant and the time spent in handling tax matters. Because of the high cost of compliance, small businesses may decide not to comply if they perceive the benefits of compliance to be significantly lower.

3.3 Compliance Burden

PricewaterCoopers International Limited (2015) explains that governments have to understand the importance of creating a tax system that is efficient and easy to comprehend in order to promote compliance with tax laws. A tax system that is cost effective brings about many benefits such as economic growth; taxpayers comply with laws and more income is generated, which in turn promotes economic growth. According to the Small Business Administration Office (2011), compliance burden is the amount of time and money that taxpayers forgo every year in order to comply with tax laws. There are various factors that can influence compliance burden such as accessibility to information, the cost of compiling the information and the level of difficulty in computing tax documents.

Ma (2015) states that high level of compliance burden is a result of having a complex tax system. The problem becomes more prominent in cases where the country is using a self-assessment system. The burden of ensuring full compliance with tax laws is shifted on the taxpayer, therefore leading to other issues such as intentional or unintentional non-compliance with tax laws. Lignier and Evans (2012) further add that modern tax systems are known to be quite burdensome on small businesses. They explain that tax burden comprises of three main elements. Firstly, it is the tax itself and how it is being imposed on small businesses (whether on the profit or the turnover). Secondly, there are efficiency costs, also known as deadweight losses, which are market distortions that have been induced by taxes. Thirdly, the tax system has operating costs, meaning the administrative costs of complying with tax laws. This is often referred to as compliance costs.

3.4 Complexity of Tax Laws

McKerchar (2007) explains that a tax system is one that is complex if there is an excessive demand for keeping records, completing tax forms or any other burdensome obligation faced by a taxpayer. The author further identifies some factors of complexity in tax laws to be "... black letter law, grafting of legal meaning, tax reform, differentiated taxation of entities, policy framework, the progressivity of the personal tax system and the desire to address equity concerns".

By looking at some of the above factors, it can be said that there are some that might be contributing to the complexity of tax laws in the Republic of Seychelles. Firstly, the country underwent tax reforms in 2009 and the reform is still ongoing, the Presumptive Tax regime for small businesses is still new since it was introduced in 2013, some sections of tax laws are unclear and no proper interpretation is provided and finally, there is the question on whether the government is doing enough to address equity issues. The author insists that the presence of such factors would certainly create complexity in tax laws, thus leading to high level risk of non-compliance on the part of taxpayers.

4. Conceptual Framework

The study involved establishing the relationship between the tax system and the level of compliance with tax laws. The Economic Theory of Tax Compliance developed by Allingham and Sandmo (1972) was modified and used in this study. It comprises originally of the three existing elements (tax rates, tax audits and tax penalties) and modified to include a fourth variable, which is record keeping. We conceptualize the independent variable as the tax system and the dependent variable as compliance with tax laws. However, the framework does not take into consideration other elements of the tax system such as filing of registration, filing of returns, tax payments, taxpayer education and so on. We believe that the tax system in the Republic of Seychelles will influence the level of small business compliance with tax laws.

4.1 Independent variable

In this conceptual framework, the tax system is the independent variable. Although there are more elements falling under the tax system, for the purpose of this study, only a few will be discussed. The tax system includes the tax rates, record keeping of tax documentation, undergoing tax audits and facing tax penalties. Inasius and Nusantra (2015) and the GIZ Sector Programme Public Finance (2010) support the argument that there is a positive relationship between the tax system and the rate of compliance with tax laws. This means that having a weak tax structure and poor policy management and administration can directly impede compliance with tax laws, and consequently the collection of revenue.

4.1.1 Tax rates

The works of Allingham and Sandmo (1972), Fischer et al (1992) and Mas'ud et al (2014) support the suggestion that tax rates will influence taxpayers' decision to comply with tax laws. The authors argue that high tax rates contribute to non-compliance with tax laws, in the sense that they cancel out their perceived overpayment by evading taxes (e.g. declare lower income). However, other studies such as that of Modugu et al (2012) conclude that there is no relationship between tax rates and tax compliance. The mixed results in this area proves that further investigation in the field is required in order to come to a conclusion for the case of the Republic of Seychelles specifically. For the purpose of this study, the impact of tax rates on compliance will depend on whether businesses perceive the rates to be fair or not. Mas'ud et al (2014) and Barbuta-Misu (2011) argue that if taxpayers perceive the rates to be unfair, the higher the level of non-compliance. Based on the above discussion the hypothesis is stated here as:

Ho: 1.There is a positive relationship between tax rates and the rate of compliance with tax laws.

4.1.2 Record keeping

One of the obligations of businesses is to maintain accurate and up-to-date records of all their financial transactions and other tax-related documents. Guyton et al (2004) suggest that poor record keeping on the part of taxpayers will ultimately lead to non-compliance with tax laws. This is because it will have a direct impact on their income declaration as well as their ability to submit their return and make payment on time. Guyton et al (2004) explain that small businesses have to complete several activities when it comes to record keeping such as obtaining and organizing records, prepare reports for tax purposes, double check entries to ensure accuracy of information and identifying and correcting mistakes. The authors further argue that in their study, record keeping was rated as the most burdensome obligation of compliance, therefore making record keeping a potential compliance burden for taxpayers which has to be further investigated. Based on the above discussion the research hypothesis is stated here as:

Ho: 2.There is a positive relationship between record keeping and the rate of compliance with tax laws.

4.1.3 Tax audits

Modugu and Anyaduba (2011) describe audit activities as being important in increasing voluntary compliance. The works of Barbuta-Mitsu (2011) explains that if a taxpayer believes that there is a high probability of being audited, he / she will be more likely to comply with tax laws. On the other hand, if the audit probability is low, the rate of non-compliance is more likely to increase. Studies conducted by Evans et al (2005), Niu (2010) and Tagkalakis (2013), establish that there is a positive relationship between tax audit and voluntary compliance. Therefore, including audit as a probable variable influencing tax compliance proves to be very crucial. Based on the above discussion the null hypothesis is stated here as:

Ho: 3.There is a positive relationship between tax audits and the rate of compliance with tax laws.

4.1.4 Tax penalties
According to Doran (2009), Allingham and Sandmo's (1972) standard deterrence model suggests that taxpayers are likely to comply with taxes if they perceive the penalties to be higher than the cost of compliance. In a self-assessment system such as that of the Republic of Seychelles, the collection of taxes is highly dependent on voluntary compliance. Theory suggests that the strict imposition of penalties, non-compliance could be greatly reduced as proven by Doran (2009), Brbuta-Mitsu (2011) and Maciejovsky et al (2001). Therefore, it is important to include tax penalty as a factor influencing tax compliance in this particular study. Based on the above discussion the null hypothesis is stated here as:

Ho: 4.There is a positive relationship between tax penalties and the rate of compliance with tax laws.

4.2 Dependent variable
In this conceptual framework, tax compliance has been identified as the dependent variable. Tax compliance involves how a business operates in relation to the tax system; whether the business is respecting what the tax authority is expecting of them. The Republic of Seychelles depends a lot on voluntary tax compliance especially more with the introduction of the self-assessment system. Studies from various authors such as Allingham and Sandmo (1972) and Fischer et al (1992) suggest that the tax system itself, coupled with the opinions of taxpayers will influence the level of compliance with tax laws. This study seeks to establish whether this is the case for small businesses in the Republic of Seychelles.

The OECD (2001) proposes a method in which compliance can be measured in studies similar to this one. The use of questionnaires in sample surveys can assist a researcher in capturing several variables that taxpayers feel can cause them to be non-compliant. In this case, the study seeks to understand their position in terms of tax rates, their record keeping obligations, audit probability, the risk of facing severe penalties and whether any of these would influence their decision to comply. However, OECD also adds that the validity of the response may be compromised for fear or shame of admitting to being non-compliant. On the other hand, Hessing et al (1988) established that taxpayers would be very willing to share their views and opinions as long as their identity remains unanimous.

5. Methodology
Data was collected from 360 small businesses coming from 12 different business sectors. A questionnaire was used comprising of Likert type questions, whereby respondents were asked to rank their responses as 1= Strongly Disagree, 2= Disagree, 3= Neutral, 4= Agree and 5= Strongly Agree. The tax system comprised of four variables, namely tax rates, record keeping, tax audits and tax penalties. The summated scores for each variable was computed and measured against the scores for compliance.

5.1 Data reliability
The cronbach alpha method was used to determine the reliability of the data collected. That is, it was done to test the level of consistency in the data collected. The acceptable score for cronbach alpha is 0.70. The results of the test can be seen in Table 3. The results vary from 0.813 to 0.916, proving that the data used for this study is reliable.

Table 3: Reliability Test

VARIABLES	NUMBER OF MEASUREMENT ITEMS	CRONBACH'S ALPHA
Tax rates	4	0.813
Record keeping	4	0.877
Tax audits	4	0.903
Tax penalties	4	0.916
Tax compliance	5	0.859

Source: Research Data, 2015

6. Research Finding and Results
The findings on the relationship between the tax system and compliance levels were measured using data gathered from the questionnaire. The data collected aimed to answer the main research question: How does the tax system influence compliance with tax laws? In order to understand more about the characteristics of the respondents, we first of all provide their demographic characteristics. The next step was to measure data for each variable against data on compliance in order to understand the strength of the relationships. The Pearson Correlation Coefficient was used to carry out this test.

6.1 Respondent rates
A pilot study was first conducted with a total of 15 small businesses and the final questionnaire was distributed to another 360 respondents. Respondents were randomly picked using their Taxpayer Identification Number (TIN) from the Client Management Software and the SPSS software. A total of four employees conducted the survey by visiting each business. The response rate for the survey was 100%, thus proving the effectiveness of the method used.

7. Major Findings
7.1 Relationship between tax rates and tax compliance
It was found that there is a positive relationship between these two variables. When asked if they believe the tax rate is fair for all businesses, 81% of the respondents were not in favor. This could be due to bigger businesses under the normal business tax having the opportunity to declare their expenses and if their profit falls below SCR 150,000, they are liable to 0% tax. On the other hand, small businesses are taxed on their turnover rather than their profit; therefore they pay 1.5% tax, no matter their expenses and whether they made a loss. When asked if tax rates would influence their decision to comply with tax laws, 44% of the respondents thought so. It is important therefore to seek more understanding of taxpayers' grievances in this area and come up with ways to mitigate the risks of evasion. Table 4 below represents the responses in relation to tax rates from the questionnaire.

Table 4: Relationship between tax Rates and Tax Compliance

	Strongly agree	Agree	Neutral	Disagree	Strongly disagree
Tax rate is fair for all taxpayers	3%	7%	9%	33%	48%
Tax rates are not too high for small businesses	4%	21%	32%	31%	12%
A reduction in tax rates would result in more people paying taxes	11%	26%	20%	31%	13%
Tax Evasion because of the tax rates	8%	27%	23%	31%	13%

Source: Researcher 2015

7.2 Relationship between record keeping and tax compliance
Again, the study concluded that indeed there is a positive relationship between record keeping and tax compliance. 61% of the respondents believed that record keeping is not an easy task and it consumes a lot of their time. Another 61% believed that SRC demands in terms of record keeping are too burdensome. Furthermore, 66% have the opinion that the SRC does not provide them with sufficient time to compile their records and meet their obligations. Table 5 provides the respondents' opinions of record keeping. After noting what small businesses feel in terms of record keeping, it is clear that this responsibility is very burdensome for them, thus the need to review some of these obligations and make is easier for them to comply with tax laws.

Table 5: Relationship between record Keeping and Tax Compliance

	Strongly agree	Agree	Neutral	Disagree	Strongly disagree
Record keeping is easy and not time consuming.	4%	17%	18%	32%	29%
Record keeping brings many benefits to my business.	3%	26%	38%	29%	4%
SRC does not impose many demands in terms of record keeping.	4%	18%	18%	55%	6%
SRC provides me with sufficient time to compile my records.	6%	23%	5%	56%	10%

Source: Researcher 2015

7.3 Relationship between tax audits and tax compliance

The findings of the research conclude that there is a positive relationship between tax audits and the level of tax compliance. 51% of respondents believed that the probability of being audited is low, compared to only 29% who believed it is high. Believing that it is improbable that they would be selected for an audit would undoubtedly drive non-compliance. Furthermore, 38% believed that even when undergoing an audit, the probability of being detected is low. To make matters worse, 46% of respondents agree that it is worthwhile to understate their income. This clearly shows that there is some deficiency in audit activities conducted by the SRC, and this matter requires immediate attention. Failing to do so will worsen the level of compliance. Table 6 below shows the data collected from the questionnaire in regards to tax audits.

Table 6: Questionnaire responses in relation to tax audits

	Strongly agree	Agree	Neutral	Disagree	Strongly disagree
a) The probability of being audited is high.	5%	24%	20%	40%	11%
b) It is not worthwhile to understate my income	6%	31%	17%	38%	8%
c) The likelihood of being detected is high when being audited.	10%	12%	40%	27%	11%
d) All businesses at one point undergo auditing.	11%	21%	27%	33%	8%

Source: Researcher 2015

7.4 Relationship between tax penalties and tax compliance

The analysis concluded that the relationship between tax penalties and tax compliance is one that is positive. This means that the higher the penalties, the higher the levels of compliance. In the case of the Republic of Seychelles, the opinions of small businesses portray ineffectiveness in tax penalties, thus resulting in low levels of compliance. 47% of small businesses were not aware of tax penalties in place to combat non-compliance. 54% believed that penalties are not being strictly enforced by the SRC and 66% believe that the penalties in place are not strict enough to prevent non-compliance. Another 54% were of the opinion that the SRC is unfair in issuing penalties. More detail is provided in Table 7 below. The responses show that penalties issued by the SRC are not serving their intended purpose of preventing non-compliance, which is why compliance levels are rapidly decreasing. It is a must for the SRC to address this issue in order to further promote compliance.

Table 7: Questionnaire responses in relation to tax penalties

Percentage	Strongly agree	Agree	Neutral	Disagree	Strongly disagree
Taxpayers are aware of the penalties that exist.	13%	26%	15%	33%	14%
Penalties are being strictly enforced for non-compliant behavior.	12%	22%	14%	41%	13%
Penalties are strict enough to prevent non-compliance.	9%	21%	11%	53%	6%
SRC is fair in issuing penalties	6%	19%	20%	39%	16%

Source: Researcher 2015

8. Hypothesis Testing

The hypothesis of the study was tested using the Pearson Correlation Coefficient. This was used to assist in determining the strength of the relationship between the dependent and independent variables. Table 8 shows that all variables have a value above 0, meaning that a positive relationship exists between the independent variables and the dependent variables. Therefore, all four hypotheses as indicated in Table 9 have been accepted.

8.1 Pearson Correlation Coefficient

The purpose of conducting a correlation analysis was to test the strength of the relationship between the variables. As can be seen from Table 8, there is a strong positive relationship between all independent variables (tax rates, record keeping, tax audits and tax penalties) and the level of compliance with tax laws. The highest correlation was between compliance and tax audits (0.819), followed by tax penalties (0.805) and after that record keeping (0.774). The lowest correlation was between compliance and tax rates. Since they all have strong positive relationships, it can be said that improving the tax system will lead to improvement in tax compliance. However, in this case, the results show that the poor performance of the tax system is indeed influencing the low levels of compliance that the country is experiencing.

Table 8: Results for Pearson Correlation Coefficient

VARIABLES	AVERAGE SCORE OF TAX COMPLIANCE	
	Pearson Correlation Coefficient	Level of Significance
Average score of Tax Rates	.544**	.000
Average score of Record Keeping	.774**	.000
Average score of Tax Audits	.819**	.000
Average score of Tax Penalties	.805**	.000

It can also be noted that all variables are above 0.5, therefore implying that there is a strong positive relationship between tax rates, record keeping, tax audits, tax penalties and tax compliance. From the analysis output, it can be seen that the variables are significantly correlated since the p value is less than 0.05 ($p < 0.05$). The implication of identifying a positive relationship between all variables is that if the independent variables are in an upward trend, the level of compliance will also increase. On the other hand, if the independent variables move in a downwards trend, the level of compliance will also decrease.

Table 9: Summary of hypothesis testing

Hypothesis	P-Value	P-Value result	Decision
H1: There is a positive relationship between tax rates and the rate of compliance with tax laws.	0.05	0.01	Accepted H1
H2: There is a positive relationship between record keeping and the rate of compliance with tax laws.	0.05	0.01	Accepted H2
H3: There is a positive relationship between tax audits and the rate of compliance with tax laws.	0.05	0.01	Accepted H3
H4: There is a positive relationship between tax penalties and the rate of compliance with tax laws.	0.05	0.01	Accepted H4

Source: Researcher 2015

9. Discussion

From what was gathered in this study as can be seen in Appendix A, it is clear that the tax system has a strong influence over compliance with tax laws in the Republic of Seychelles. The results show that the low performance of the tax system is one of the factors contributing to non-compliance. Amongst the four variables analyzed, the strongest correlation was between tax audits and compliance. Businesses have the perception that the probability of being audited is low; and even if they are undergoing an audit, the probability of being detected is low. As a result, businesses view that not complying with tax laws is more beneficial than having to comply.

The second highest correlation was between tax penalties and tax compliance. First of all, it was seen that many businesses were not aware of the penalties that are being imposed by the SRC, therefore, they believe that such penalties are (i) not strict enough and (ii) not being properly enforced. Therefore, it cannot be agreed upon that penalties are being used for their intended purpose; to act as a deterrent for non-compliance. It was seen that record keeping also has a negative impact on compliance; businesses view it as a difficult and complex task. Furthermore, the results show that businesses believe the SRC imposes too many demands in terms of record keeping and provides them with insufficient time to fulfill their obligations. The end result would most certainly that business will fail to comply with what is expected from them.

Finally, tax rates had the lowest positive correlation with compliance. Businesses perceived that the rates are too high for small businesses and they are rather unfair when compared to larger businesses. A significant amount of respondents also held the opinion that tax rates would be the cause of non-compliance. This will certainly be the case, since the perception of unfairness would lead to non-compliance as seen in other studies.

Conclusion and policy implication

Generally, the results of this study have shown that there is a positive relationship between the tax system and the level of compliance with tax laws. Evidence from the SRC database shows that compliance levels are alarmingly low and this study has identified some possible issues with the tax system that could be encouraging non-compliant behaviour. Firstly, the tax rate is believed to be unfair, whereby bigger businesses could be benefiting from lower tax rates under the normal business tax regime. The purpose of having the Presumptive Tax regime was to encourage small businesses to be more compliant, but this is not turning out to be the case. The perception of unfairness could be a major deterrent of tax compliance. The government has to conduct a comprehensive analysis of the Presumptive and the normal Business Tax regimes and redesign the regimes as deemed necessary. Respondents of the study believe that taxes are unfair, possibly because of the gap between the two regimes. The government will have to align these two regimes to ensure that businesses falling under the lower end of the normal business tax are not paying significantly lower taxes compared to the businesses in the higher end of the Presumptive Tax regime. Businesses in the Presumptive Tax regime are taxed on their turnover; therefore, their expenses are not taken into account when computing their tax liabilities. Different business activities will have different levels of expenditure; for example, the service sectors will most probably incur lower expenditures than businesses in the manufacturing or retail sectors. Therefore, there is a need to differentiate between business sectors and the type of expenses they make. Businesses can continue being taxed at the standard rate (1.5%), but the government can also introduce a standard deduction rate depending on the sector under which the business falls. Instead of opting to move into the normal Business Tax Regime to declare their expenses and as a result face more compliance burden (e.g. record keeping, tax computation, hiring technical experts), small businesses can also be offered standard deductions in the Presumptive Tax Regime.

Secondly, most respondents perceived their record keeping requirements to be too burdensome. The positive relationship between record keeping and tax compliance can be further illustrated by the very low compliance levels recorded by the SRC. Once again, the Presumptive Tax regime has not met its intended purpose of simplifying taxpayers' obligations in terms of record keeping. The SRC should assist small businesses with their record keeping obligations by conducting unannounced on-site verification visits to ensure small businesses are keeping their records as required by the law. In cases where gaps are identified, SRC officers should provide them with proper guidance on record keeping and allow them enough time to correct their mistakes. If the business fails to do so, the SRC can issue penalties for breaching the law.

Effective tax audits have proven to be very good a measure of discouraging non-compliance, but this has not been the case for the Republic of Seychelles. According to the data collected, respondents perceive tax audit activities to be ineffective. As previously mentioned, failing to have properly executed audits especially in a self-assessment system (as is the case for the Republic of Seychelles), can motivate taxpayers to be non-compliant. The government needs to recognize the crucial role that SRC auditors play in improving compliance with tax laws. There has to be an understanding that compliance will continue to decline if the severe issue of having an under-staffed audit unit is not addressed immediately. The SRC should be allocated more funds for recruitment of audit employees in order to increase the number of audits conducted per annum. In doing so, more cases of non-compliance will be detected, non-compliant behavior will be discouraged and more revenue will be collected due to higher levels of compliance. The SRC also has to reinforce its audit capability by budgeting for training and development for audit staff. Changing legislation and taxpayer behavior coupled with a dynamic business environment will require frequent training and capability improvement. Audit employees can also undergo competency assessments to identify their strengths and weaknesses, and take necessary measures to fill in the gaps so that their skills remain up to date and relevant. Publicizing details of audit strategies can have certain legislative limitations, but the SRC can nonetheless publicize some of its audit achievements to deter non-compliance, such as making the public aware of the results of audit projects or even convictions for evasion.

Tax penalties serve the purpose of punishing non-compliance, and preventing others from acting likewise. Unfortunately, the respondents did not perceive this to be the case in the Republic of Seychelles. Their views are of the opinion that penalties are not being properly administered. The study conveyed that there is a positive relationship between tax penalties and tax compliance. Therefore, ineffective implementation of tax penalties would lead to non-compliance, as it has been seen in the Republic of Seychelles. All four independent variables measured in this study had a positive relationship with tax compliance. Therefore, if the variables are perceived to be negative in nature, the level of compliance is expected to be low. One conclusion that can be drawn is that the tax system itself is indeed causing the low levels of compliance that the Republic of Seychelles is currently experiencing. The SRC will have to review the implementation of penalties for non-compliance, since it is currently not proving to be very effective amidst small businesses. First of all, the Taxpayer Education & Service Delivery and Enforcement units have to work jointly to raise awareness on the types of penalties that exist for non-compliant behavior. This can be done through weekly articles in newspapers, brochures focusing on penalties or a specific location on the SRC website listing all penalties that exist. To address the issue of unfair penalties, the SRC has to carefully analyze the conditions under which penalties are issued; they have to ensure that taxpayers do not face penalties in circumstances whereby the law is ambiguous / unclear of what is expected of the taxpayer. A careful review of existing legislation is required and necessary amendments made. Enforcement officers have to treat all businesses equally and show no sign of preference for one over another. Failing to issue penalties as stipulated by the law will encourage non-compliant taxpayers to continue with this behavior and will also discourage compliant taxpayers to continue fulfilling their tax obligations. The SRC can therefore create a database of penalties issued that can be used as reference for issuing future penalties.

References
Abdi, M. (2010). Role of Tax Audit in Improving Tax Compliance: Case of the Iranian Taxation System. http://en.intamedia.ir/pages/download.aspx?mode=document&id=194 (viewed 21st August 2015).
Allingham, M. G., Sandmo, A. (1972). Income Tax Evasion: A Theoretical Analysis. Journal of Public Economics 1(3): 323-338.
Barbuta-Misu, N. (2011). A Review of Factors for Tax Compliance. Annals of Dunarea de Jos University of Galati.
Batrancea, L., Nichita, R., Batrancea, I. (2012). Understanding the Determinants of Tax Compliance Behavior as a Prerequisite for Increasing Public Levies.The USV Annals of Economics & Public Administration 12 (2): 201-210.
DeLuca, D., Greenland, A., Guyton, J., Hennessy, S., Kindlon, A.(nd).Measuring Tax Compliance Burden of Small Businesses. {HYPERLINK "http://www.irs.gov/pub/irs-soi/05deluca.pdf"} (viewed 2nd September 2015).
Doran, M. (2009). Tax Penalties and Tax Compliance.Harvard Journal on Legislation, 46: 111-161.
Evans, C., Carlon, S., Massey, D. (2005).Record Keeping Practices and Tax Compliance of SMEs.eJournal of Tax Research, 3(2): 288-334.
Fischer, C., Wartick, M., Mark, M. (1992). Detection Probability and Taxpayer Compliance: A Review of the Literature.Journal of Accounting Literature, 11: 1-46.
Gambo, E., Mas'ud, A., Nasidi, M., Oyewole, O.(2014).Tax Complexity & Tax Compliance in African Self-Assessment Environment. International Journal of Management Research & Review,4 (5): 575-582.
GIZ Sector Programme Public Finance (2010).Addressing Tax Evasion and Tax Avoidance in Developing Countries. DeutscheGesellschaft fur, Germany.
Guyton, J., Kindlon, A. Zhou, J.(2004). Recent Research on Small Business Compliance Burden. {HYPERLINK "http://www.irs.gov/pub/irs-soi/04kinnta.pdf"} (viewed 2nd September 2015).
Hessing, D., Elffers, H.,Weigel, R.(1988). Exploring the Limits of Self-Reports and Reasoned Action: An Investigation of the Psychology of Tax Evasion Behaviour. Journal of Personality and Social Psychology, 54: 405-419.
Inasius, F., Nusantra, B.(2015).Tax Compliance of Small and Medium Enterprises: Evidence from Indonesia. Accounting and Taxation, 7(1): 67 – 73.
International Finance Corporation (2007). Designing a Tax System for Micro and Small Businesses: Guide for Practitioners. World Bank Group.
International Monetary Fund (2015).Current Challenges in Revenue Mobilization: Improving Tax Compliance.IMF Working Paper.
International Monetary Fund, Organization for Economic Development and World Bank (2011). Supporting the Development of More Effective Tax Systems. Working Paper.
Kwai Fatt, C., Wong Sek Khin, E. (2012). Disclosure of self-assessment tax systems on Malaysian agriculture based industries. Journal of Development and Agricultural Economics, 4(13): 361 – 370.
Lignier, P., Evans, C. (2012). The rise and rise of tax compliance costs for the small business sector in Australia. Australian Tax Forum, 27: 615-672.
Ma, D. (2015).Small Business Tax Compliance Burden: What can be done to Level the Playing Field?.Msc thesis, University of Canterbury.
Maciekovsky, B., Kirchler, E., Schwarzenberger,H. (2001). Mental Accounting and the Impact of Tax Penalty and Audit Frequency on the Declaration of Income – An Experimental Analysis. {HYPERLINK "http://edoc.hu-berlin.de/series/sfb-373-papers/2001-16/PDF/16.pdf"} (viewed 2nd September 2015).
Mas'ud, A.,Aliyu, A,Gambo, E. (2014). Tax Rate and Tax Compliance in Africa. Journal of Accounting Auditing & Finance Research, 2(3): 22-30.
McKerchar, M. (2007).Tax Complexity and its Impact on Tax Compliance and Tax Administration in Australia. Proceedings of the 2007 IRS Research Conference, University of New South Wales.
Modugu, P., Eragbhe, E., Izedonmi, F. (2012). Government Accountability and Voluntary Tax Compliance in Nigeria. Research Journal of Finance & Accounting, 3(5): 69-76.

APPENDIX 2: SAMPLE PUBLISHED PAPER 2

Full Length Research Paper

Financial sector reforms in bank ownership and its impact on service quality case of commercial banks in Tanzania

Lucky Yona[1]* and Eno Inanga[2]

[1]Eastern and Southern African Management Institute P.O. Box 3030, Arusha, Tanzania.
[2]Maastricht School of Management, Endepolsdomein 150 6229EP Maastricht, the Netherlands.

Accepted 9 December, 2013

The purpose of this study was to determine the impact of change in bank ownership on competitiveness of commercial banks in Tanzania in the aspect of service quality. The study adopted a service quality (SERVQUAL) model to determine the impact of financial sector reforms on bank ownership and its impact to service quality of commercial banks in Tanzania. Customers were randomly selected from thirty two commercial banks in Tanzania that were already registered by year 2010 following the financial sector reforms. Self-administered questionnaires were distributed to 1600 participants. Of these, 893(60%) responded. Data were analyzed using SPSS 17.0 to estimate the mean score of service quality dimensions as well as to determine the association between reforms on bank ownership and service quality dimensions. Majority of semi quasi banks customers disagreed that banks offered good service quality to customers as compared to private banks based on the five dimensions of service quality. In terms of tangibility, semi-quasi banks had higher mean (SD) scores as compared to private banks (2.50(1.053) vs. 2.23(0.8790, p= 0.001) respectively. We found Similar observation in terms of reliability [(2.87(1.125) vs. 2.64(1.016, p=0.012)], assurance [(2.85(1.121) vs. 2.67(1.008) P= 0.046)]. However there was no significance difference in terms of empathy between the two groups [(3.28(1.156) vs. 3.43(1.176), p=0.098)]. In terms of responsiveness majority of the participants agreed that banks offered good service quality with a mean score (SD) of 4.00(1.028) and 3.97(0.982) p= 0.723 for semi-quasi and private banks respectively. Overall, financial sector reforms on bank ownership was shown to have no major impact on all service quality dimensions except for responsiveness. In concluding the research it was found that financial sector reforms is positively associated to all service quality dimensions except for service quality empathy.

Key words: banking competitiveness, financial sector reforms, bank ownership, service quality, Tanzania.

INTRODUCTION

Immediately after her independence Tanzania economic performance was good, except in the mid 1970's where the economic performance declined which led to severe macro-economic imbalances in the country, and this had negative effect on the performance of the financial sector. This in the end undermined the contribution towards economic recovery. The Nyirabu Commission report (1988) indicates the reasons for the financial sector reforms in Tanzania. The objectives of the reforms included the reforming of the commercial banks so as to increase competition, diversify ownership and financial restructuring, reforming development finance institutions so as to expand a pool of resources available for investment, reforming other financial institutions so as to improve customer services and ensuring financial viability ,integrity and sustainability. It was therefore formulated to review the structural, organization procedures, operational arrangements and policy issues related to financial system. The review revealed number of problems related to structural, business and policy environment as well as managerial deficiencies which undermined the

---

*Corresponding author. E-mail: yona_lucky@yahoo.com Tel: +255 754 499307

performance of the financial sector. According to BOT (2007) financial sector reforms in Tanzania included the enactment of the banking and financial institution of 1991, which paved the way for licensing of new banks and financial institutions resulting into greater competition in the financial sector. All these reforms aimed at improving the performance and competitiveness of banks for enhancing economic development of Tanzanian economy. The objectives of the financial sector reforms undertaken by Tanzania do not differ so much with those objectives of other countries in the world as identified by Bonacorris and Handy (2005) study.

The banking sector in Tanzania started during the era of colonialism, characterized by domination

of commercial banks. Kimei (1987) reports that during the of Germany rule there were only two banks commercial banks in Tanzania, one in Dar-es-salaam (Ostrifikanshe Bank) which started in 1905 and Handel bank of Ostafrica established in 1911. During the British era, after the first world war in the 1950's, three commercial banks were established namely National Bank, Standard Bank and Barclays Bank which later were followed by other foreign banks such as the India bank and Bank of Baroda in 1954 and thereafter in the 1960's more foreign banks such as the National Bank of Pakistan and the Ottman Bank. Bagachwa (1995) argues that the nationalization of private properties following the socialist policy in 1967 led to entire change in ownership of the banks by the state. The banks that were there at that time included the central bank and three commercial banks, all of them owned by the state. These banks were not subject to competition and lacked adequate supervision. The banking system during this time was subject to financial repression, geared towards the provision of cheap credit to central government, state enterprises and cooperatives. The bank of Tanzania acted as the lender of first resort. In this period, banks made large losses due to poor management, inadequate supervisions, auditing and legal protection for both debtors and creditors. Following the reforms on ownership of Banks and liberation of bank entry, Tanzania witnessed a many banks coming to Tanzania. By the end of year 2010 the banking sector comprised of thirty two banks (32) (Appendix: Table 1) majority being private banks from foreign and three banks local banks which have mixed ownership (Private/Government/Public).

Statement of the problem

Prior to financial sector reforms in Tanzania, the banking sector was considered to be poor or weak in service delivery simply because of monopolistic types of banks which led to laxity and lack of competition among the banks. Customers had no option of receiving different banking services except from few state owned banks that existed at that time. Despite the fact that these were public banks they were also few, located only in major cities, they were characterized with monopolistic nature of providing services, lacked adequate number of staff who could provide quality services to customers. These banks were also underperforming in terms of profitability and had few innovations on financial services that could help to provide good quality services to bank customers. The financial sector reforms that the government of Tanzania initiated in the mid-nineties had number of objectives that aimed to enhance the performance of these banks by allowing the entry of new banks from the private sector which led to the mushroom of new banks majority of these banks being foreign banks. Looking carefully at the objectives of financial sector reforms on bank ownership, there is no clear guidelines on how these banks could have addressed the provision of quality services to customers and hence the improvement of competitiveness among the commercial banks. There is also inadequate literature evidence to show whether the financial sector reforms on bank ownership has led to any impact on the improvement of quality services provided by these commercial banks. General studies that provide a link between what influences service quality of commercial banks do not real provide the answer and therefore a need to be substantiated by this type of study that intend to link the reforms on bank ownership and service quality. The inadequate empirical evidences of such studies in Tanzania are the motivation factor to undertake the study which answers the research questions: To what extent financial sector reforms on bank ownership affected the banking competitiveness in respect to service quality of Tanzanian commercial banks?

LITERATURE REVIEW

Financial sector reforms

Empirical studies by various researchers suggest proper justification of financial sector reforms in different countries especially developing countries like Tanzania. However, studies also show that the objectives of financial sector reforms vary from one country to another. According to Seck and Eli-Nil (1993) Kenya for example adopted the reforms in order to improve banking regulations and legislation which led to introduction of new financial institutions and new financial instruments contrary to Zaire which introduced the reforms in order to develop measures that could sustain money and government securities markets. Levin (1997) argues that financial sector reforms aims at enhancing competitions in the financial sector especially in countries where financial institutions including banks are state owned.

Ngugi and Kabubo (1998) on their study on financial sector reforms in Kenya argued that the government took financial sector reform measures to remove policy and institutional constraints in the operation of treasury bills and Treasury bond markets. Other objective of the reform was to strengthen the legal and technical capacity of the central bank to carry out its regulatory and supervision function. Martin (1999) argued that the objectives of the reforms in most developing countries were to build more efficient, robust and deeper financial systems, which could support the growth of the private sector enterprises. Martin continues to argue that financial liberalization is normally intended to stimulate greater competition in the banking markets through two entry channels; new entry by private sector banks to challenge the oligopolistic market position of the established public sector and the removal of administrative constraints on competition such as interest rate controls. Barth et al. (2003) argue that financial sector reforms have the aim of restructuring the state owned financial institutions through privatization and lowering the barriers for entry of international financial institutions in order to make the financial sector more competitive and efficient, which could facilitate greater economic development and growth. Inanga and Ekpenyong (2006) argues about three different objectives as to why many African countries opted to financial sector reforms. First, there are those countries whose objective was to improve their monetary control systems such as Botswana and Mauritius. Secondly there are countries which introduced financial sector reforms in order to improve mobilization and allocation of domestic savings. The World Bank Study (2007) in East African countries supports these arguments as the study revealed that the objectives of the financial sector reforms aim at encouraging savings mobilization and allocation.

However, a different study by Silvanus and Abayomi (2001) on financial sector reforms, macroeconomic instability and order of economic liberalization in Nigeria do not suggest any positive benefit of the financial reforms. In their study, the financial sector reforms in Nigeria began in 1997. Since then the reforms, which included the chartering of new banks, capital markets reforms, deregulation of interest rates have been disappointing. The implementation of the reforms led to bank insolvency, high inflation and interest rates, which was the sign that the health of the bank deteriorated following the reforms in Nigeria.

Silvanus and Abayomi (2001) continued to argue that the implementation of the financial reforms were accompanied by variable rates of inflation and increased number of problem banks and suggested that the reasons for this phenomena was the improper timing and wrong sequences of the Nigerian reform policies. Lastly, there are countries whose financial sector reforms objectives were to improve the banking systems and structure of interest rates. Typical examples of those countries include Mauritania, Senegal, Burundi and Gambia. Contrary to expected benefit of financial sector reforms on various countries as discussed above Chandavakar (1992) argues that financial liberalization has not always brought about the maximum expected benefits in least developed countries due to few innovations in financial markets and limited competitiveness, while Stiglitz (1994) argues about the impact of information imperfections on market failure which at the end it has negative impact on liberalization.

It obvious that various countries have undertaken the financial sector reforms with the aim of improving the financial systems, improving country financial resources mobilization, improving banking systems, regulations and competitiveness for the betterment of the overall country economic development.

Banking competitiveness

The competitiveness of the banking sector falls under competitiveness of the firm. A competitive bank is defined as the bank that produces sustainable future high returns to its shareholders. However, other definition from perspectives of other groups might be different from this definition. Competitive bank by the government banker is different from customer or manager perception, Government banker define banking competitiveness as the bank that achieves maximum safety in payment system, efficiency in credit allocation and responds to monetary and fiscal policy changes while customers view a competitive bank as the one which can provide customers with highest paying deposits, lowest interest loans, cheapest and best financial services. Managers of a bank may define a competitive bank as giving high salaries and benefits and offering expanding opportunities for safe career advancement (Thomas and Chancing, 2006).

Arai and Yoshino (2000) in their discussion paper on concept of competitiveness in the financial sector they explained four major broad issues that underlie competitiveness of individual financial institutions , which include efficiency, size , information technology and resources management. Each of these issues is measured by specific indices, which represent comparative advantage of the financial institutions. Mourihno and Phillips (2002) argued that one of factors that can have great influence on bank competitiveness is high emphasis on strategic planning of the banking system. Hauswald and Marquez (2002) looked at financial sector competitiveness in terms of availability of better information technology. They argued that information technology may lead to improved information processing, lower costs of financial intermediation and lower costs of information.

Other variables that are considered to affect bank competitiveness include financial power, market share, human capital, international exchange activities and use of technology (Givi et al., 2010). However, their study in Iran revealed that financial power was the most powerfully effect on bank competitiveness.

Beverly (1991) study on competitiveness of interntional financial institutions argued that banks and securities firms compete successfully in international markets by building on strengths which include the existence of an established customer base, technical expertise and innovative ability resulting from specialization in particular domestic market. Competiveness success depends on size of the institution and capitalization. Size of the institution helps to determine whether the bank can take advantage of economies of scale while capitalization may affect institution credit standing. Besanko and Thankor (1992) argued about benefits of banking competitiveness as the results of relaxing the bank entry barrier which allows more banks to join the industry. In their theoretical model they concluded that relaxing bank entry barrier allows heterogeneity in products and can lead to decline in loan rates and increased deposit interest rates. The study concluded that increased interbank competition might induce banks to make more relationship loans but Stain (1997) study results showed that when there is severe competition in the financial market there are benefits in allocating capital more efficiently.

Bin Wen (2004) argues about three competitiveness factors, which play a vital role in the banking
sector. These are financial technology, organizational structure and human resources. While studying the four state owned banks in China he found that the core competitiveness factors of Industrial and Commercial bank of China was the provision of E-Service, for the construction bank was provision of comprehensive services and for the Bank of China it was foreign exchange business.

Service quality

While service quality is considered to be an indicator of competiveness, Heshelt et al. (1994) define it as the measure of how well a delivered service matches customer's expectations. Since banks compete in market place with generally undifferentiated services and products then service quality becomes a key competitive weapon (Stafford, 1999). Service quality is defined as the kind of services offered to customer that meets the demands/needs of customers. Other definition is that service quality is that service offered to give customer satisfaction. Parasuraman et al. (1988) defined service quality as the customer judgment of overall excellence about services quality. This judgment has sole foundation on the difference that what is expected from customer from the service provider and what the actual services the customer receives from it. Other definition by Roth and Van der Velde (1991) perceived service quality as a drive for retail banking. Heshelt et al. (1994) clarifies the role of quality as they argued that profits and growth are stimulated by customer loyalty while loyalty is the direct result of customer satisfaction while satisfaction is largely influenced by the value of services provided to customers, value is created by loyal and productive employees and employee satisfaction results primarily from high quality support services and policies that enable employees to deliver results to customers. Alshammari (2006) study adopted three levels of measuring service quality that commercial banks can offer to their customer. The first level is on measuring the desired service level (the level of service that a customer believes that excellent bank can and should deliver), second is measuring the adequate service level (the minimum level of service that the customer considers acceptable) and lastly measuring the perception of individual customer of bank performance as well as the perception of customers on banks policy on customer focused policies and product differentiations. In other words service quality is a customer satisfaction indicator.

CONCEPTUAL FRAMEWORK

Service Quality as an indicator of competiveness is considered to be the services that banks can offers to their customers. The SERVQUAL model measures the gaps between customers' expectations and customers' perception on service quality. On each of these criteria there are questionnaires which customers are expected to answer and thereafter establish the gap between customer's expectation and perception. We adopt the SERVQUAL model of service quality to describe customer perception on change of service quality as the result of financial sector reforms on bank ownership. However we have ignored the expectation side of customers and adopted only the five service dimensions used by SERVQUAL model to measure customer's perceptions. SERVQUAL covers five dimensions that are considered by a customer in evaluating perceived quality services in a service sector such as a bank. Parasuraman et al. (1988) and Van laarden et al. (2003) grouped service quality into five dimensions to include Tangibility, Reliability, Respon- siveness, Assurance and Empathy We conceptualize the independent variable as reforms on Bank ownership and service quality dimensions as our dependent variables. We believe that the reforms on banks ownership could influence the ways banks deliver services to its customers as banks.

Independent variable

The independent variable of this study is the reforms on bank ownership. Private ownership of banks and semi-quasi ownership (Mixed or private) is likely to influence the service quality of a commercial bank. The reforms that took place in Tanzania changed the ownership of the state owned banks to semi-quasi banks and new private banks emerged thereafter.

Bank ownership

Ownership of banks vary from private ownership, state ownership and semi-quasi ownership. In this study we pick private banks and semi-quasi banks because after the financial sector reforms in Tanzania all state owned banks were privatized. Private Banks are those banks which are wholly owned or privately controlled by individuals apart from the state. This was not the case for commercial banks in Tanzania prior to the financial sector reforms. Prior to financial sector reforms in Tanzania all commercial banks were state owned. According to Hansel and Sachin (1995) private banks are only concerned with profits and hence likely to neglect public services while public sector banks are assumed to have broader social objective in mind and hence likely to offer quality services to customers. Kangi and Voukelatos (1997) study concluded that private banks have similar profile of expectation of service quality as those in public banks while customer perception of the services offered were superior in private banks. In support of these, Madanmohan (1999) argues that private banks lead to increased customers' expectations regarding customer services. Bank customers tend to believe that private banks believe that customer is the king and should be given better treatment.

Panigraphy (2000) argues that entry of private banks can lead to bank opening the door to customers with new options for service. However Lynn, Lytle and Samo (2000) concluded that private banks outperform public banks in both service orientation and financial performance. In respect to entry of private banks, Kangi and Kareklis (2001) argue that public and private banks behave and deal differently with their customers and employees though public banks are likely to be under control, more bureaucratic usually more honest and less concerned with profits. Entry of privates banks have revolutionized the way in which banks depart from monopolistic banking operations to competitive operations. Sureshchandar et al. (2003) argue private banks kindle competitive spirit within public banks but public banks are less concerned with quality services in relation to diversity and range of services offered. Thierno et al. (2005) study on impact of change in ownership on bank efficiency in Asian countries during the post Asian crisis period 1999-2004 concluded that banks privately owned perform better than state owned banks. Based on these theoretical arguments, the following main hypotheses were stated as follows:

Ho: 1. Change in bank ownership is negatively associated to Service Quality
H1: 1. Change in Bank ownership is positively associated to service Quality

In this research we also test the following minor hypotheses

Ho.1a: Change in bank ownership is negatively associated to service quality in terms of tangibility
Ho.1b: Change in bank ownership is negatively associated to service quality in terms of reliability
Ho.1c: Change in bank ownership is negatively associated to service quality in terms of responsiveness.
Ho.1d: Change in bank ownership is negatively associated to service quality in terms of Assurance.
Ho.1e: Change in bank ownership is negatively associated to service quality in terms of Empathy.

Dependent variable

Our dependent variables is banking competitiveness as measured by service quality dimensions namely tangibility, reliability, responsiveness, empathy and assurance. These variables were discussed as follows:

Tangibility

Apart from Parasaranman et al. (1988) who defined tangibility as appearance of physical facilities, dressing well of employees and having written materials that are visually appealing .Anath et al. (2011) defined tangibility as modern looking equipment, physical facilities, dressing well of employees and having materially that are visually appealing. Other scholars have defined tangibility as the surroundings represented by objects and subjects appearance of employees who plays a major role in meeting customers' needs and bringing customers satisfaction from the service delivered. According to Heshelt et al. (1994) tangibility is measured by looking whether the service provider has up to-date equipment's, physical facilities are visually appealing, having bank employees are well dressed and appear neat and whether the appearance of the physical appearance is in keeping with the types of service. Following the financial sector reforms on ownership customer expected that both private banks and semi-quasi banks tangibility of services would improve to bring high quality services

Reliability

While Roth (1991) define reliability as the ability of the service provider to provide accurate and dependable services to customers, Van (2003) defines as the ability to perform the promised services dependably. There is a link between reliability and customer satisfaction that is why Jayajaraman et al. (2010) study on service quality in the banking sector in Malaysia concluded that reliability has no significant effect on customer satisfaction.

Responsiveness

Responsiveness, according to Van (2003) means the willingness to help customers and provide prompt services. According to Anath et al. (2011) responsiveness can be established by measuring whether a bank employees do tell customers exactly when services will be performed, whether customers receive prompt service from banks employees, bank employees are willing to help customers and whether bank employees of bank are too busy to respond to customer requests promptly.

Assurance

Assurance according to Van (2003) means the ability, competence, courtesy, credibility and knowledge of employees. Assurance also refers to the knowledge and courtesy of employees and their ability to inspire trust and confidence to customers as they provide services. In measuring the degree of assurance of banks employee to customers we can measure whether bank customer can trust employees, whether customers feel safe in transacting with bank customers and whether employees get adequate support from Bank to do their

Empathy

Empathy according to Van (2003) means access, communication, understanding the customer. It further includes the caring and providing individualized attention that the firm provides to its customers. According to Parasaranman *et al.* (1988) establishing customer empathy banks have to be tested whether bank employees provide individualized attention and care to the customers and whether bank's employee do not know what are the individual customer needs and whether the bank employees do have best interests of customers at heart.

METHODOLOGY

We collected data from customers of Tanzanian Commercial banks that were existing by the end of year 2010 .We collected information from customers of the 32 commercial across four regions in Tanzania, namely Mwanza, Arusha, Kilimanjaro and Dar-es-salam where majority of customers of these banks are situated. These regions are also considered to have many economic activities leading to the desire of bank services by people. The research questionnaires used in this study were on 5 likert scale requiring customers and bank officials to rank their responses as 1= strongly disagree, 2= Disagree, 3= Neutral, 4= Agree and 5=Strongly Agree. A total number of one thousand six hundred (1600) questionnaires were distributed to bank customers and only 838 (60%) questionnaires were returned by customers. The questionnaires to customers adopted the SERVQUAL model of service quality (With minor variation) to analyze customer perception on change of service quality as the result of financial sector reforms. SERVQUAL covers five dimensions that are considered by a customer in evaluating perceived quality services in a service sector such as a bank. Parasuraman *et al.* (1988). Van laarden *et al.* (2003) grouped service quality into five dimensions to include Tangibility, Reliability, Responsiveness, Assurance and Empathy. Because of nature of the data we describe the perception of customers on these variables by obtaining the composite scores of service quality dimension indicators through a transformation process. These variables indicators are then measured by the use of a five likert scale indicators ranging from one to five, where 1 is equated to strongly disagree, 2 equated to disagree, 3 to neutral, 4 equated to agree and 5 equated to strongly agree. This is achieved by computing the summated scores of these variable indicators to obtain one score indicator for all variables and then the frequency distribution table was run.

Data reliability

Cronbach alpha was used to determine the reliability of service quality dimensions. Reliability is normally measured by using cronbach's alpha test. The rule of thumb is that the value of Cronbach's alpha should be >0.5 to give confidence of relying on the data. If Cronbach alpha is < 0.5 then it is conclude that there may be variable indicators which are not reliable for measuring service quality and therefore a need to conduct a factor reduction analysis. Reliability results are presented in Table 1. The coefficient results range from 0.512 to 0.873.This shows that our variables are reliable for testing our data and therefore no need of carrying further statistical test and removing any questionnaires from the study.

RESEARCH FINDINGS AND RESULTS

The finding on relationship between reforms on bank ownership and competitiveness in terms of banks service quality is measured by the responses from the questionnaires from bank customers. We first analyze data to obtain answers on the following research question: To what extent financial sector reforms on bank ownership affected banking competitiveness in terms of Service quality? In order to answer the research question and understand the relationship between financial sector reforms on bank ownership and service quality dimensions we first give the findings on demographic characteristics and we then calculated the mean scores and standard deviation for each of the service quality variables namely tangibility reliability, responsiveness, assurance and empathy for two groups of banks namely private and semi-quasi banks.

Demographic characteristics

The study targeted a population of one thousand six hundred (1,600) customers from all commercial banks designed for the study but the response was eight

Table 1. Reliability scores of service quality dimensions.

Service Quality Dimension	Items	Reliability Score (α)
Tangibility	4	0.873
Reliability	4	0.793
Responsiveness	4	0.696
Assurance	4	0.512
Empathy	4	0.768

Source: Researcher 2013

Table 2. Mean scores and standard deviation -service quality.

Service quality dimension	Bank ownership	N	Mean(SD)	P-value
Tangibility	Private	209	2.23(0.879)	0.001
	Semi quasi	625	2.5(1.053)	
Reliability	Private	208	2.64(1.016	0.012
	Semi quasi	618	2.87(1.125)	
Responsiveness	Private	205	3.97(0.982)	0.723
	Semi quasi	600	4.00(1.028)	
Assurance	Private	210	2.67(1.008)	0.046
	Semi quasi	610	3.43(1.176)	
Empathy	Private	207	3.43(1.176)	0.098
	Semi quasi	617	3.28(1.156)	

hundred and thirty eight customers (838) which is almost sixty percent (60%) of the total population. According to the results (Appendix: Figure 1) responses came from customers of both private banks and semi-quasi banks. Of all customers' responses, 25% were customers from private banks and 75% from semi-Quasi banks. In terms of bank locations majority of customers (Appendix: Figure 2) were from Kilimanjaro (56%), Arusha (14%), Dar-es-salaam (19%) and Mwanza (10%). As far as gender is concerned (Appendix: Figure 3) majority of respondents were male (61%) and female were thirty seven percent (37%). The respondent's age group (Appendix: Figure 4) ranged from age of 18 years to sixty years (60) while majority had the age between 18 and 29 years (48%), between 30 years and 40 years 30 (30%), between 41 years and 50 years (13%),between 51 years and 60 Years (6%) and above 60 years (2%). In terms of customer length of relationship with the bank Appendix: (Figure 5), 33.5% of the bank customers had stayed with the bank for a period between 1-3 years, 31% a period between 4-6 years, 7-10 years and 13% a period between 11-20 years. Customers level of deposits (Appendix: Figure 6) ranged from those customers with less than Tanzanian Shillings 100,000 (16.8%), Tanzanian Shillings 100,000-500,000 (10%), Tanzanian Shillings 501,000-1,000,000 (10%), Tanzanian Shillings 1,000,001-999,000,000 (10%) and Tanzanian shillings (1,000,000,000 and above (10%) Mean Scores and Standard Deviation. According to Table 2, individual scores on Tangibility show that semi-quasi banks have high mean (SD) scores of 2.50 (1.053) as compared to private banks with mean scores of 2.23(0.879) at significance level of p-value 0.001. On reliability semi-quasi banks have high mean (SD) scores of 2.87(1.125) and private banks have mean (SD) of 2.64(1.016) at significance level p-value of 0.012. Semi Quasi banks have high mean (SD) scores of 4.00(1.028) on responsiveness and private banks have mean (SD) scores of 3.97 at p-Value 0.723 which is not significant. The results on assurance indicate that semi-quasi banks have high mean (SD) scores of 2.85(1.121) as compared to private banks which have mean (SD) scores of 2.67(1.008) at significance level of P-values 0.046 and results on empathy indicate mean (SD) Scores on semi-quasi banks are 3.28(1.156) which are lower than the mean (SD) scores of private banks which are 3.43(1.176) at significance level of p-value of 0.098. This means that generally we can conclude that private banks are doing much better than the semi-quasi banks in all areas of service quality except on empathy.

BIBLIOGRAPHY

1. Aveyard, H. (2010). *Doing a literature review in health and social care: A practical guide* (2nd ed.). Berkshire, Great Britain: Open University Press.
2. Allan S and Kenneth R (2008): *The importance of External Validity:* AM Journal of Public Health 98(1), 9-10
3. Attride-Stirling J. (2001). *'Thematic networks: an analytic tool for qualitative research'.* Qualitative Research, vol. 1, no. 3: pp. 385–405 [Online]. Available at http://goo.gl/VpQeQJ (retrieved on 19 Aug 2019).
4. Chenail R, Duffy M, Sally G and Dan W (2011) *Facilitating Coherence across Qualitative Research Papers.* The Qualitative Report Vol 16 No 1 263-275
5. Crossman, Ashley (2020) *"How Intervening Variables Work in Sociology."* ThoughtCo, Feb. 11, 2020, thoughtco.com/intervening-variable-3026367.
6. Creswell, J. W. (2005). *Educational Research:* Planning, Conducting and Evaluating Quantitative and Qualitative Research (2nd Ed.). Pearson Merrill Prentice Hall.
7. Daneil Udo-Akang, (2012). *Theoretical Constructs, Concepts, and Applications.* American International Journal of Contemporary Research, 2(9).
8. David W and Peter W (2003). *Using Research Instrument, A practical Guide for Researcher*: Taylor and Francis e-Library
9. DeMunk V.C and Sobo E.J (1998). *Using Participatory Methods in the field: a practical introduction and casebook.* Walnut Creek, CA, Atlanta Mira Press.
10. DeWalt K, DeWalt B (2002). *Participant Observation in guide for field Workers.* Walnut Creek, CA, Atlanta Mira Press.
11. Everitt, B. S. (2002). *The Cambridge Dictionary of Statistics* (2nd ed.). Cambridge UP. ISBN 0-521-81099-

12. Gilbert A, Churchil Jr and Dawn I (2002). *Marketing Research, Methodolical Foundations;* 8th Edition. Thomson learning publication
13. John D(2018) *The Ultimate Guide to Writing a Dissertation in Business Studies:* A Step-by-Step Assistance- E-Book
14. Yona L (2016). *The impact of Bank ownership on Banking competitiveness in Tanzania.* Maastricht Institute of Management
15. Yona L & Inanga E (2014). *Financial sector reforms in bank ownership and its impact on service quality.* Case of Commercial banks in Tanzania. Journal of Business Administration and Management Science Research. Vol 2 (12), pp 335-351
16. Magigi W and Kazungu I (2016): *Data Analysis and Research Report* (3rd Edition): Safi Publishers Co Ltd.
17. Majid U (2018). *Research fundamentals: Study design, population, and sample size.* URNCST Journal. 2018 Jan 10: 2(1).
18. Merriam S.B (1998) *Case study research in education: a qualitative approach.* San Francisco: Jossey -Bass Publishers.
19. Mohammad Z(2013) *Mixed Method Research: Instruments, Validity, Reliability and Reporting* Findings Theory and Practice in Language Studies, Vol. 3, No. 2, pp. 254-262,
20. Galvan, J. L. (2013). *Writing literature reviews:* A guide for students of the social and behavioral sciences. Glendale, CA: Pyrczak.
21. John (2018) *The Ultimate Guide to Writing a Dissertation in Business Studies:* A Step-by-Step Assistance **January 2018 edition**
22. J FLEMING (2018): *Work-integrated learning research methodologies and methods Methodologies, methods and ethical considerations for conducting research in work-integrated learning,* International Journal of Work-Integrated Learning, Special Issue, 2018, 19(3), 205-213
23. Persaud, N. (2010). Primary data source. In N. Salkind (Ed.), Encyclopedia of research design. (pp. 1095-1098). Thousand Oaks, CA: SAGE Publications, Inc.
24. Petty, R. E., Briñol, P., Loersch, C., & McCaslin, M. J. (2009). The need for cognition. In M. R. Leary & R. H. Hoyle (Eds.), Handbook of individual differences in social behavior (pp. 318–329). New York, NY: Guilford Press.
25. Pope, C., Ziebland, S., and Mays, N. (2000). 'Analyzing qualitative data'. British Medical Journal, 320: pp. 114–116
26. Shamoo, A.E., Resnik, B.R. (2003). Responsible Conduct of Research. Oxford University Press.

27. Kabir and Seyid Basic Guidelines for Research: An Introductory Approach for All Disciplines, Edition: First, Chapter: 9, Publisher: Book Zone Publication, Chittagong-4203,
28. Richards, J. C. & Schmidt, R. (2002). Longman dictionary of language teaching and applied linguistics. Third ed. London: Longman.
29. Thatcher, R. (2010). *Validity and Reliability of Quantitative Electroencephalography.* Journal of Neurotherapy, 14, 122-152.
30. Willis, J. (2007). *Foundations of Qualitative Research: Interpretive and Critical Approaches.* SAGE Publications.
31. Yona L (2016). The impact of Bank ownership on Banking competitiveness in Tanzania. Maastricht Institute of Management
32. Jachi M, Yona L (2019). *The Impact of Professional Competence & Staffing of Internal Audit Function on Transparency and Accountability Case of Zimbabwe Local Authorities:* Research Journal of Finance and Accounting: Vol 10, No 8 (2019) pg. 154- 164
33. Jachi M, Yona L (2019) *The Impact of Ethics & Objectivity of Internal Audit Personnel on Transparency & Accountability Case of Zimbabwe Local Authorities.* European Journal of Business and Management. Vol.11, No.7, 2019 pg 108-124
34. Yona L and Inanga E (2017): *The impact of Bank Ownership Structure on Bank Growth: Case of Tanzanian Commercial Banks.* Research Journal of Finance and Accounting; Vol 8, No 4(2017), pp 80-96
35. Yona L and Inanga (2017) *Bank ownership structure: Influence on Economic Efficiency of Commercial Banks; Case of Tanzanian Commercial Banks.* Journal of Economics and Sustainable Development, Vol 8, No 6, p68-81

ALSO, BY LUCKY YONA

Chief Executive Officers and Managers require a range of skills and knowledge to be able to function effectively in their positions. This book is a guide for holders of these positions, examining the varied facets of management and leadership along with the techniques necessary to make effective day-to-day decisions and improve the performance of their organizations

This book is intended to be used as a textbook in Financial Accounting for Executive MBAs candidates. This book has simplified the subject matter and gives understanding that can be easily applied by Executives as they try to manage their organizations. The author believes that this book will meet the needs of Executives who study Financial Accounting as a module in their course. The book is presented in a simple language which will make the subject not only interesting but also enjoyable for the learners.

This book is intended to be a textbook in International Finance. As a textbook, it covers most of the theories and concepts in the field, clearly explaining concepts and theories with practical application to developing countries environment and can help students to understand how international finance concepts are applicable in the business world. The author believes that this book will meet the needs of students undertaking MBA courses in International Business and Trade and other professional courses such as CPA, CIMA CFA and ACCA. The presentation of this book is in a simple language, which makes the reading interesting and enjoyable to both students and managers in this field.

This book is intended to bridge a gap on non-availability of Corporate Finance textbooks. In order to respond to this need, the book has been developed to provide reading materials in various topics on Corporate Finance. The book is intended to be used as a textbook as most of the theories and concepts in the field are clearly explained with practical mathematical calculations that clearly help to understand how the concepts are applicable in the business world. The author believes that this book will meet the needs of students undertaking MBA courses and other professional courses in CPA, CMA CFA and ACCA. The book is presented in simple methodology which will make Corporate Finance interesting, enjoyable and will provide both students and managers in the field with understanding of the subject matter.

This book is all about public finance and contemporary issues in taxation. The book discusses about contemporary issues in taxation that cater across all developing countries as well as discusses the concept of public debts and balance of payments. These are related issues that are critical for the economic development of a country. Students undertaking their undergraduate studies, postgraduate studies, and professional studies will find the book to be useful and full of knowledge in the various issues that affect taxation in their countries.

The dominant capital structure studies across the globe have been concentrated in developed countries and specifically for listed companies and few on unlisted companies or mixed companies. This thesis aims to examine the extent to which company liquidity, profitability, tangibility, and company size influence the leverage of Tanzanian companies as suggested by pecking order and trade-off theory. The study findings show a negative relationship between company liquidity and company leverage as measured by debt ratio and debt-to-equity ratio. These findings show the validity of the pecking order theory in Tanzania. The postulates of the trade-off theory as far as liquidity is concerned are not valid. The study findings also reveal a positive relationship between profitability and leverage, suggesting that majority of Tanzanian companies used more debts as the means of financing their business operations despite their profitability. The study also found that the tangibility of listed companies was higher than that of the unlisted companies and that there was a negative relationship between tangibility and leverage, which is valid to pecking order but contrary to trade-off theory. As far as company size is concerned, study findings suggest that pecking order theory (POT) and trade-off theory (TOT) relevance cannot be fully supported in Tanzanian companies as the findings have revealed a negative relationship between company size and leverage. Findings reveal a negative relationship between company size and leverage. Pecking order theory (POT) and trade-off theory (TOT) relevance cannot be fully supported in Tanzanian companies, and size of listed companies was higher than that of the unlisted companies. This suggests that the size of majority of Tanzanian unlisted companies is still small as compared to the listed companies

This book is all about foreign direct investment (FDIs) in the context of Malawi as one of those African countries which their FDI'S growth is at low pace. The book discusses about the FDIs in selected economic sectors in Malawi namely mining, agriculture, insurance, banking and telecommunication. The book has also discussed about the factors that determine the FDIs in respective sectors as well as the impairing factors and has tried to highlight the key recommendations for improvements that can enhance FDIs growth in Malawi.

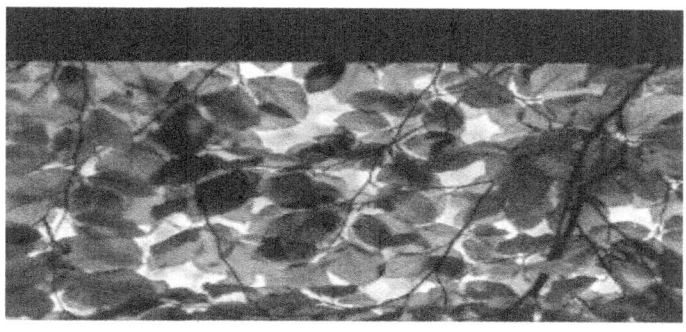

Foreign Direct Investment
Selected Economic Sectors in Malawi

Printed in Great Britain
by Amazon